COLOSSIANS

Joyce Meyer's Biblical Study Series

Ephesians
James
Galatians
Colossians

COLOSSIANS

A Biblical Study

JOYCE MEYER

FaithWords

NEW YORK NASHVILLE

FaithWords
Hachette Book Group
1290 Avenue of the Americas, New York, NY 10104

faithwords.com

twitter.com/faithwords

First Edition: March 2020

FaithWords is a division of Hachette Book Group, Inc. The FaithWords name and logo are trademarks of Hachette Book Group, Inc.

The publisher is not responsible for websites (or their content) that are not owned by the publisher.

The Hachette Speakers Bureau provides a wide range of authors for speaking events. To find out more, go to www.hachettespeakersbureau.com or call (866) 376–6591.

Library of Congress Cataloging-in-Publication Data has been applied for.

ISBN: 978-1-5460-2614-3 (hardcover); 978-1-5460-2613-6 (ebook); 978-1-5491-8423-9 (downloadable audio)

Printed in the United States of America

LSC-C

10 9 8 7 6 5 4 3 2 1

CONTENTS

HOW TO READ THIS BOOK

I suggest that you take your time studying this book. Don't just skim over the book so you can finish it quickly. Take your time, not only reading but also pondering what you read. Stop at places that are important to you; think about how they apply to you personally and whether or not you need to make changes in your life in order to comply with God's will.

Answer the questions you will find at different places in the book because they will help you recognize areas in which you need to grow.

I also suggest that you take the time to look up the Scripture references throughout the book. Space did not permit us to print out each one, but you can open your Bible to the references mentioned and read the Scripture passages for yourself. The effort you put into doing this will enhance your overall experience with the book. Another option is to read the book in its entirety and then reread it in the manner I have suggested.

Remember that studying is different than simply reading. When we read, we take in information, but when we study, the information becomes revelation to us—it becomes part of us and affects our lives and behavior in deeper ways than a quick reading does.

ABOUT COLOSSIANS

Author: *Paul*
Date: *Around AD 61*
Audience: *Christians in the city of Colossae*

When I first began thinking about this Biblical Study series, I wondered, "Are these books resources that people will really be interested in?" I concluded that they could help people greatly because the Bible—especially the New Testament and certain Old Testament books—is full of practical answers for everyday living.

The Bible is more than a book about theology or a story about eternal life when we die. It also offers us the wisdom we need to live victorious, peace-filled, joyful lives on earth. Jesus says in John 10:10, "The thief comes only in order to steal and kill and destroy. I came that they may have *and* enjoy life, and have it in abundance [to the full, till it overflows]" (AMP). This verse is not only talking about enjoying life when we go on vacation or when something delightful happens. John 10:10 is talking about the fact that God offers us the ability to relish ordinary, everyday life. If the only time we can enjoy ourselves is when something exciting happens, we will miss out on the joyful, abundant life Jesus died to give us. But if we learn to live according to God's Word, which requires study and obedience, we can savor each day.

Any time we familiarize ourselves with the Scriptures, it is good for us. But we need to do more than simply read God's Word; we need to study it deeply. We may read only one verse or passage for several days, but if we are really examining it and digging deep to understand what it means in our lives, that's when it will begin to transform us. The Bible teaches and empowers us in amazing ways, and we can only discover them when we diligently study it.

Most of the New Testament letters, called the Epistles, were written to young churches and believers who needed to grow in their faith and learn to live God's way. The writers—including the apostles Paul, James, Peter, and John—were trying to help new believers become established in their relationship with God and learn how to live godly lives. That's why they contain not only valuable theological principles but also important advice for our practical, everyday lives. I am excited to know that I will one day go to heaven, but I also want to enjoy the life I have today and every day before I go there.

One reason Paul's epistle to the Colossians is so important for us to study and understand is that it is *all about Jesus*. From start to finish, this letter exalts Jesus and affirms His lordship. The theme of the epistle is the headship of Christ, and the primary lesson of these four chapters is to put Jesus first all the time, above and before everything else. We are to put Him first in our time, finances, thoughts, conversations, decisions, and relationships. If we keep Him first, we will never have to strive for or chase after anything. The blessings of God will chase us and overtake us (Deut. 28:2).

In Matthew 6:31, Jesus spoke about people who do not keep Him first and the fact that they worry about their lives, saying, " 'What shall we eat?' or 'What shall we drink?' or 'What shall we wear?' "

He went on to say that people who do not know God "run after all these things," but that "your heavenly Father knows that you need them" (Matt. 6:32).

Then He said: "But seek *first* his kingdom and his righteousness, and all these things will be given to you as well" (Matt. 6:33, emphasis mine). When we keep Jesus first and seek His kingdom above all else, we can live in love, peace, joy, power, and blessing.

Paul's letter to the Colossians focuses so intensely on Jesus and encourages us to keep Him in first place in our lives because Paul knew that the believers in Colossae had been exposed to a false spiritual teaching that said Jesus was not really God. This popular belief system of the day, called Gnosticism, questioned Jesus' lordship, sufficiency, and supremacy. At the time Paul wrote Colossians, Christianity would have been in jeopardy of being completely overwhelmed by false religions had God's grace not protected it. He understood the extreme danger this heresy presented to the Christians in Colossae and responded to it strongly with this epistle, emphasizing the importance of exalting Jesus over everything else. Out of his love and care for them, he confronted the heresy in this letter so they would realize how harmful it was to their faith and would be able to stand against it.

Gnosticism is a strange mixture of all kinds of different so-called religions, including Jewish legalism, Greek philosophy, and Eastern mysticism, all interwoven in a most cunning and deceptive way. 2 Thessalonians 2:7 refers to this as "the mystery of lawlessness" (AMP). Gnosticism teaches that human beings cannot know God. I cannot imagine anything sadder than for a person to be committed to a religion, diligently practicing it day after day, week after week—and to know they will never have a personal connection with the god they worship. As Christians, we believe that Jesus did not die for people to subscribe to a religion but for us to have a personal, intimate relationship with God.

While Gnostics say human beings cannot know God, Christians believe knowing God is the central theme and goal of life. Gnosticism is filled with human reasoning and is therefore attractive to the human mind. But it is satanic in origin. Some scholars even believe what was going on in the church of Colossae was the root of what is called Christian Science today. The purpose of Paul's letter to the early Christians in Colossae was to urge them to beware of such deception and hold fast to Jesus as Lord.

Paul wrote his letter to the Colossians while he was in prison in Rome around the same time he wrote to the Ephesians and the Philippians. He had never been to Colossae or met the believers there. Most likely, a man named Epaphras, who was probably the leader of the church at Colossae and had converted to Christianity under Paul's ministry, asked Paul for his help. Though Paul did not know the people in the church personally, he cared about them and wanted to help them combat Gnosticism and strengthen them in their faith.

His letter to the Colossians defends, explains, and promotes the lordship of Jesus Christ more than any other book of the New Testament. One reason Colossians matters so much right now is that we are living in a day when we are not encouraged to put God first. In fact, some people are mocked or even persecuted for doing so.

We don't hear the word *Gnosticism* used to reflect what is happening in our contemporary society. But like the Colossians, we, too, are faced with false teachings that aim to cause us to stray from God with mixtures of theologies and philosophies that can leave us feeling confused and empty.

Another reason Paul wrote to the Colossians was to instruct the early believers in how to walk in this world as a Christian—a follower of Christ who lives in personal relationship with Him—in practical ways. The first chapter of Colossians alone includes twelve different lessons that will help you enjoy your life and stay strong in your faith each day. You may not be able to incorporate all of them into your life right away, but if you choose a few of the ones that seem most important for you and study them and apply them to your life, they will help you mature and live the life Jesus died for you to live.

Other highlights of Colossians include but are not limited to:

- The fact that we have been rescued from darkness and forgiven of sin (Col. 1:13–14)
- The truth that we are reconciled to God through Christ and can live in right relationship with Him (Col. 1:21–23)
- Paul's powerful teaching that Christ in us is the hope of glory (Col. 1:27)
- The reminder that Christ has reconciled us to God and that in Him we are complete, lacking nothing, and fully forgiven (Col. 1:22; 2:10, 13)
- Paul's comments on the importance of representing God well by being compassionate, kind, humble, gentle, patient, and loving toward others (Col. 3:12–14)
- The instruction to let the peace of God rule in our hearts (Col. 3:15)
- The exhortation to do everything as though we are doing it for God, not for other people (Col. 3:23)

My prayer for you as you make your way through this book is that Jesus will become more real to you than ever, and that Paul's devotion and passion for Jesus will inspire you to love

Him and walk with Him even more closely than you already do, putting Him first in every area of your life.

Key Truths in Colossians:

- Jesus deserves first place in every area of our lives, and putting Him first should be a priority for us (Col. 1:15–20).
- Jesus' victory on the cross empowers us to overcome spiritual darkness and confusion (Col. 2:15).
- We are to set our minds on the things that have eternal value and keep them set on them, not allowing our thoughts to waver (Col. 3:1-4).
- The words of our mouths are powerful, and they are to be filled with grace (Col. 4:6).

DISCOVERING AND PURSUING GOD'S WILL

An Overview of Colossians 1

Colossians chapter 1 is one of the most powerful chapters in the New Testament. It includes Paul's greeting to the Colossians, which is more meaningful than a casual reading of it would suggest, and twelve key lessons for anyone who wants to grow spiritually. Learning and applying all these lessons could take years, but if you choose just a few to start with and focus on them over and over again and begin practicing them, they will transform your life and keep you on the path toward spiritual maturity. I will elaborate on each one in my commentary on their corresponding verses, but I am listing them here for you so you can begin to see what a powerful chapter Colossians 1 is.

1. The most important thing you can do in your practical, everyday life is to make sure you are living in the will of God (Col. 1:1).
2. Living holy lives should be our goal (Col. 1:2).
3. Being thankful can change your life and make every day better (Col. 1:3).
4. Focusing on your faith and living by it—trusting God no matter what—will keep you spiritually strong (Col. 1:4).

5. Love is what distinguishes believers from those who do not know Christ, and we are to live lives of love (Col. 1:4).

6. Whatever you do, hold on to your hope and do not let the devil steal it (Col. 1:5).

7. Paul's apostolic prayer will help you understand all that belongs to you in Christ, and it is a life-changing way to pray for yourself and others (Col. 1:9–12).

8. We have everything we need in Christ (Col. 1:13–14).

9. Jesus is before and above everything else. Put Him first (Col. 1:15–18).

10. Christians can rejoice in suffering (Col. 1:24).

11. Part of the Christian life involves being willing to be a servant to God and others (Col. 1:24–25).

12. Christ in you is the hope of glory, and Paul's goal was to present every believer mature in Christ (Col. 1:27–28).

Colossians 1 is filled with insight and revelation for your life. Many people, myself included, have studied this chapter for years and are still finding new treasures and spiritual strength in it. I pray the same will be true for you.

Personal Reflection

Which lessons from Colossians 1 do you believe you need most in your life right now?

_____

_____

_____

_____

_____

_____

_____

The Importance of Being in God's Will

Colossians 1:1

Paul, an apostle of Christ Jesus by the will of God, and Timothy our brother.

Colossians 1:1 is a short verse, but as we study it carefully, we realize that it is packed with meaning. Notice first that Paul says he is "an apostle," which in this case simply means a person sent by God. Next we see that Paul is an apostle "of *Christ Jesus*" (emphasis mine). This is important because it tells us that Paul is serving God, not himself or other people. Before Paul met Jesus on the road to Damascus (Acts 9:1–9), he was known for the zeal with which he persecuted Christians. He did everything he could to stop the cause of Christ. Once God touched him and changed his life, he poured all of his energy into loving Him and building His kingdom. The greatest fulfillment in life comes from belonging to God. And the best way we can spend our lives is to be in His will, enjoy being in a personal relationship with Him, serve Him, and help others know and grow in Him.

Notice also that Paul is an apostle "by the will of God." This is important because, as Christians, we want to follow God's will. If we are not doing what we do because we truly believe it's God's will for us, how can we ever do it well or enjoy it?

Many times when I teach about being in the will of God, people ask, "How can I know if I am in the will of God?" Here are two simple ways:

1. You will enjoy it.

I mentioned John 10:10 in the introduction to this book. It tells us that Jesus came so that we may "have *and* enjoy life, and have it in abundance [to the full, till it overflows]" (AMP). God's will for you will not be something that makes you miserable all the time. You may face challenges as you pursue it, or you may be required to make sacrifices, but if it is God's will for you, He will give you the wisdom and grace to overcome any difficulty. And I believe you will enjoy the work you do in serving God.

2. You will be equipped for it.

I believe that when what we are doing is in the will of God, we will be good at it. God gives us the skills, gifts, and abilities to fulfill His will for our lives. He does not call us to do something without equipping us for it.

You may have to work, study, or prepare in some other way to carry out His call on your life, but you will have an aptitude for it and feel at ease in it. I have become very comfortable doing what I do as a teacher of God's Word. I have learned some lessons about doing it effectively, and I do work at it, but teaching is not hard for me because I teach by the will of God.

Think about a woman who is called and designed to be a stay-at-home mom. If that is what God wants her to do, but she tries to do something else because she thinks it is what she needs to do to be a modern woman, she will be miserable. She needs to know what God's will is for her life and put her time and energy into *that*, as well as being a wife and mother. It may sound like a daunting task, but God can enable you to do whatever He wants you to do.

My hope for you is that you reach the point where you can say, "I want to do what God wants me to do. I'm not going to compare myself with anybody else. I won't compete with anybody else. I just want to be in my place doing what God wants me to do."

Finding God's will for your life is not difficult: You step out and try things until you find what is comfortable for you. "Comfortable" doesn't necessarily mean easy. You will likely have to work at it, but you will know in your heart that it is what you are supposed to be doing, and it will bring you peace and joy.

Taking risks and walking by faith are necessary as you seek to discover God's will. When you take a step of faith, you must be willing to be wrong in order to find out if you are right. Sometimes we are excessively bothered by the idea of being wrong, but that is part of the way we learn. When we realize we need to change direction, we can simply say, "I thought that was what God wanted. I stepped out. I tried it, but it's not right. I can check that off my list and go on to the next thing." Being in the will of God is much more important than trying to avoid being wrong.

When I first sensed God's call on my life, I believed His will was for me to serve Him, but I didn't know exactly what He wanted me to do. I wanted Him to use me, so I started saying yes to every opportunity that came my way. I went to work in the church nursery, and after only a week or two I knew that was not the place for me. I also tried street evangelism, and while I realize the value of that work, I did not have the grace to do it. I tried to be a secretary to my pastor, but after one day, he told me it wasn't working and it was not the right spot for me. When I began to teach God's Word, I found my place. Teaching is what God called, equipped, and anointed me to do, and in pursuing my calling, I am in the center of His will for my life.

God's will for your life will not be the same as His will for other people's lives. If we compare our gifts or callings with others', or if we feel guilty that we struggle to serve God in ways that come easily to others, we will not produce good fruit for God's kingdom. It's important for each person to determine what His will is for them and then pursue it wholeheartedly.

The key lesson of Colossians 1:1 is to believe that whatever you are doing is God's will for you at that time in your life. Over the course of your life, certain things may change. God's will for you today may not be His will for you ten years from now. For example, for many years when our ministry hosted conferences, I spoke in five sessions every weekend. Then I started speaking in only four sessions. Recently, I began to feel that it was God's will for this ministry to do three sessions. This has proven to be the right scheduling decision for us, and people have responded positively to the change. Being continually in God's will requires us to be willing to make changes when God leads us to do so.

Also in Colossians 1:1, Paul mentions that Timothy is with him. He thinks of Timothy as his "true son in the faith" (1 Tim. 1:2). He knew Timothy's mother and grandmother as women of "sincere faith" (2 Tim. 1:5). He invested time and energy in Timothy and apparently cared about him, believed in him, and earnestly wanted him to succeed. He wrote 1 and 2 Timothy to encourage him as a young minister. At many times during his ministry, Paul made an effort to train and encourage young ministers, and we should also be willing to do that as God leads us. Timothy was one of those young men in whom Paul invested, and you can read more of Paul's instructions and advice to him in 1 and 2 Timothy.

Personal Reflection

Do you believe that what you are doing in your life right now is in the will of God? How has God led you to that conclusion?

_____

_____

_____

_____

_____

_____

CHAPTER 2

PAUL'S HEART FOR BELIEVERS

Belonging to God Completely

Colossians 1:2

To God's holy people in Colossae, the faithful brothers and sisters in Christ: Grace and peace to you from God our Father.

Sometimes we skim past verses such as Colossians 1:2, but I want to call your attention to some important words and ideas in it. Paul says he is writing to "God's holy people in Colossae." In the Amplified Bible, Classic Edition, this reads "To the saints (the consecrated people of God) and believing *and* faithful brethren in Christ who are at Colossae: Grace (spiritual favor and blessing) to you and [heart] peace from God our Father." When we see words in Scripture such as *saints* and *consecrated*, we may skip over them because we do not fully understand what they mean. When that happens, we miss the lessons we should gain from certain verses, words, or phrases.

The words *holy people* in the New International Version (NIV) are translated *saints* in the Amplified Bible, Classic Edition and described as "consecrated people of God." To be consecrated to God means to be set apart for a special use. This is important because it teaches us that from God's perspective, when He saves us, we belong to Him. We have been saved *out* of something so we can come *into* something—out of a low life into a high life, out of a selfish, self-centered life where we just live to please ourselves into a life of serving others and being vessels through which God can do what He wants. He is the head; we are the body. In other words, He gives the direction for our lives, and we should obediently follow it.

God Works through People

The idea of being consecrated so God can use us is significant because when He wants to accomplish something, He works through people. When we pray for God to do something, He almost always works through human instruments to make it happen. Part of what makes our Christian experience interesting is letting God use us and seeing Him use others in our own lives.

Remember, to be consecrated means to be set apart for a special use, and all believers can be used by God. Instead of thinking pastors, Bible teachers, or worship leaders are the only ones God can use, know that God can use you, too. *You* are consecrated. *You* are set apart for God's use. There is something only you can do the way you can do it, and it is important to God's plan that you find what that is and start doing it.

Obviously, God will accomplish what He wants to accomplish. If you and I don't do our part, He will find someone else to do what is needed. But I believe one of the keys to being happy and fulfilled is to be in the will of God, surrendered to Him, making ourselves available for Him to use as He sees fit.

As believers, we do not belong to ourselves, and the things we call "ours" do not truly belong to us either. We were bought with a price (Christ's life), and we belong to God. His Spirit lives in us. Paul writes in 1 Corinthians 6:19–20: "Do you not know that your bodies are temples of the Holy Spirit, who is in you, whom you have received from God? *You are not your own*; you were bought at a price. Therefore honor God with your bodies" (emphasis mine).

Personal Reflection

How has God worked through the people in your life?

_____

_____

_____

_____

_____

_____

_____

Dedicate Yourself to God

Paul also writes about letting God use us in Romans 12:1: "Therefore, I urge you, brothers and sisters, in view of God's mercy, to offer your bodies as a living sacrifice, holy and pleasing to God—this is your true and proper worship." This is New Covenant thinking. Under the Old Covenant, people tried to please God with animal sacrifices. But God reached a point where He no longer wanted animal sacrifices. He wanted people with whom He could be in relationship, people He could work through—people who are full of life, take God-inspired action, and are enthusiastic and excited about life.

Every day, you can choose to dedicate yourself to the Lord as a living sacrifice. You can dedicate your eyes by being careful about what you watch and look at, your ears by being careful about what you listen to, your mouth by being careful about what you say, and your feet by being careful about where you go. For example, you can choose before you arrive at your job each morning not to listen to or spread gossip or complain. You can decide before you go on a business trip that you will not do things that you would not want your family to know about.

When we belong to God and live consecrated lives, we separate ourselves from the evil things in the world and its values. People may laugh at us or reject us, but we should remain committed to God. It is important not to feel superior to them or to judge them, but to pray for them instead. God loves them just as He loves us. But part of belonging to Him means making choices other people may not like or agree with.

I encourage you to wake up every morning thinking, *I belong to God. Everything about me is dedicated to Him. God lives in me, and I live in Him. I'm in Him, and He is in me. Greater is He that is in me than He that is in the world* (1 John 4:4). *I can do all things through Christ who strengthens me* (Phil. 4:13). That kind of thinking and self-talk will help you stay connected to God and give you the courage and confidence to believe God can use you and to pursue the special purpose for which you are set apart.

Personal Reflection

What has God revealed to you about the special way He wants to use you? How are you doing your best to prepare yourself for it?

_____

_____

_____

_____

_____

_____

_____

Grace and Peace

Colossians is one of Paul's most personal letters, which is interesting because, as I mentioned in the introduction, he had never met the believers in Colossae. His love for God, however, meant that he also had a great love for God's people. And his pastoral heart inspired him to care about Christians everywhere, even if he did not have personal relationships with them.

If you or I were to write a letter to people we had never met, we might be somewhat reserved in our language and greet them with something like "Hello. I hope you are doing well." But Paul greets the Colossians the same way he greets the people in churches he knew personally, with his usual words: "Grace and peace to you from God our Father."

His greeting was more powerful than we might first realize because he extends to his readers the amazing grace of God and the peace that surpasses all understanding. Clearly, Paul wanted the Colossians to enjoy both grace and peace, and he knew they could only experience peace if they understood and knew how to receive God's grace.

I know this from personal experience, because for a long time I struggled to change things in my life. There were things about myself, others, and my circumstances that I knew needed to be different, and I tried to make that happen in my own strength. I had to learn that only God can change things for us. When we try to do it ourselves, we end up striving and frustrated—with no peace. The more I learned to stop striving and receive God's grace, the more peace I had in my life.

We can think about grace in several ways. There is grace we say before a meal, and there is the grace of a beautiful ballet dancer. But I want to focus on two ways grace applies to our spiritual lives. First, grace is God's undeserved favor. Second, grace is God's ability and power to help us do whatever we need to do in life. It makes seemingly impossible things possible, and it enables us to do difficult things with ease. Over the years I have come up with a personal definition of grace: to me, grace is God's undeserved favor and His power that enables us to do with ease what we could never do on our own with any amount of struggle or self-effort.

When I hear about people who have no peace in their lives, I feel sorry for them. No matter what else people may have—a great education, good looks, an engaging personality, power, influence, or plenty of money—it all becomes a burden unless they also have peace. I think perhaps people who do not have peace have not yet learned about living by God's grace. Salvation comes to us by grace through faith in Christ (Eph. 2:8), and we are to live our everyday lives by grace through faith, just as we were saved "by grace" through faith, if we want to live in peace. Paul understood this, and in just a few words he communicated this powerful hope to the Colossians in the very beginning of his letter to them.

Personal Reflection

How has receiving the grace of God brought peace to you?

_____

_____

_____

_____

_____

_____

Thanksgiving and Prayer

Colossians 1:3

We always thank God, the Father of our Lord Jesus Christ, when we pray for you.

Paul writes often in his letters about being thankful. He writes of it here and in other places in Colossians (2:6–7, 3:15, 3:17, 4:2), where I will elaborate more on the power of thankfulness. Here he says, "We *always* thank God" (emphasis mine). How many of us thank God at all times? I believe the best way to start and end each day is to intentionally find several things for which we can thank God. As we go through the day, we should look for all the ways He blesses us and continue to thank Him. Being consciously aware of God's blessings and being thankful are important ways to live happy lives.

Learning to live as a thankful person can change your life. We can and should thank God for everything—even the most basic things such as being able to walk, talk, see, and hear. We can be thankful that we have something fruitful to do each day and for each opportunity He gives us. We can thank Him for our families and friends and even for things like clean water and homes that are heated and cooled. Many people in the world do not have the blessings we enjoy, so we need to be grateful for everything He provides for us. We can always be thankful that we know Him and that He knows and loves us, which is the biggest blessing of all.

Personal Reflection

What are some of the things you thank God for when you pray?

_____

_____

_____

_____

_____

_____

CHAPTER 3

—◆—

FAITH, LOVE, AND HOPE

Known for Faith and Love

Colossians 1:4–8

Because we have heard of your faith in Christ Jesus and of
the love you have for all God's people—the faith and love
that spring from the hope stored up for you in heaven and
about which you have already heard in the true message
of the gospel that has come to you. In the same way, the
gospel is bearing fruit and growing throughout the whole
world—just as it has been doing among you since the
day you heard it and truly understood God's grace. You
learned it from Epaphras, our dear fellow servant, who is a
faithful minister of Christ on our behalf, and who also told
us of your love in the Spirit.

I wish the church today was famous for our faith and love, as
the Colossians were. Paul did not know the people in Colossae, but he had heard about their faith. The Amplified Bible,
Classic Edition describes faith in this verse as "the leaning of
your entire human personality on Him in absolute trust and
confidence in His power, wisdom, and goodness."

As believers, we are faith people, but what does that mean?
2 Corinthians 5:7 says, "For we live by faith, not by sight."
This means we live according to God's Word, not according
to what we see, feel, or think—or according to what other

people tell us. We are faced with the opportunity to walk by faith every day, all day long. When we choose to put our faith in God and trust Him with ourselves and everything in our lives, we enter the joy of the Lord.

More than Conquerors

People, especially nonbelievers and carnal Christians, do not always understand the life of faith. They may question us or mock us because we trust the Lord. Paul writes about this in Romans 8:36–37: "As it is written: 'For your sake we face death all day long; we are considered as sheep to be slaughtered.' No, in all these things we are more than conquerors through him who loved us."

Our faith makes us more than conquerors. Most of us know what a conqueror is, but what does it mean to be *more than a conqueror*? I think people who are more than conquerors know they have the victory in every situation before the trouble ever starts. People who live that way do not fear trouble or dread difficulties. No one likes trouble, but those who have the attitude that they are more than conquerors can say, "Whatever happens today, whatever comes my way, I am going to get through it with God. It may be hard, but I'm going to get through it and enjoy victory. Right now it may look like I am crazy for believing the Word of God. Others may think that what I believe will happen is impossible, but I have made a decision for my life: I believe God." That's what faith sounds like for someone who is more than a conqueror.

There will always be people who dismiss us or question us

because of our faith, saying, "How can you believe that?" I have decided that if I spend my whole life believing what I believe and trusting God and His Word, and then at the end of my life I find out I'm wrong, I haven't lost anything. I've been happy in my delusion. However, if a person chooses not to have faith in God and reaches the end of their life and finds out that they were wrong, that person will face eternal torment and misery. So I've made my decision. I believe God, and I pray you do, too. Live by faith, and not by sight (2 Cor. 5:7).

What Faith Is

As we continue to think about what faith is, let's look at Hebrews 11:1: "Now faith is confidence in what we hope for and assurance about what we do not see." We often miss the first word of the verse, which is *now*. Faith is for every moment of every day. It's for the present situation. I believe that God takes care of the future and that He can heal everything that has happened in the past. But real faith is always active right now.

The amplification of Hebrews 11:1 gives us further insight into what this verse means: "Now faith is the assurance (the confirmation, the title deed) of the things [we] hope for, being the proof of things [we] do not see *and* the conviction of their reality [faith perceiving as real fact what is not revealed to the senses]" (AMPC).

Thinking about that faith as the "title deed" and "the proof of things [we] do not see" helps us understand faith much better. Think about it this way. Let's say that I walked up to you in an airport and handed you the title to my car, saying,

"Here, I want to give you my car." I would not have the car with me at the airport, so you could not see it. But if I gave you the title and if you trusted my reputation as an honest person, then you would get excited immediately because you would believe you have a new car. You haven't seen the car. You haven't driven the car. And in that moment, you might not even care what color it is or how many people it seats. You would just be thinking, "Someone just gave me a car!"

This scenario is a good illustration of how faith operates.

It is the title deed of all the promises God gives to us. He has made thousands and thousands of promises, and they pertain to everything that you could ever need in life. You can believe God for them. You can choose to stop living according to what you think, what you feel, or what other people tell you. You can choose to believe God's Word and be confident by faith that everything He promises is true.

From Faith to Faith

I want to mention one more important verse about faith. Romans 1:17 says that "in the Gospel a righteousness which God ascribes is revealed, both springing from faith and leading to faith" (AMPC). In other words, it leads us to grow from one measure of faith to greater and greater measures. When we know who we are in Christ and how much God loves us because we've read and studied the Word and come to believe it, then somehow, by a miracle of the Holy Spirit, we are able to believe things that just don't make any sense to the natural mind. I believe things that would seem to make no sense at all to most natural-minded people but are completely reasonable to one who walks by faith. For example, who could have seen where I started in life and actually believed that I would be doing what I'm doing today? But I believed it, and guess what? I am doing it. It wasn't easy. It didn't happen overnight, but it happened. God spoke it to my heart. I believed and acted in faith. And it happened. The same opportunity is available to you if you act on it.

When we stop and think about what faith really is and what it means in our lives, we can see why Paul praised the Colossians for their faith in Christ.

Personal Reflection

In what ways has your faith grown since you first started walking with God?

_____

_____

_____

_____

_____

Love for All Believers

Paul had also heard about the Colossians' love for all believers. Jesus says in John 13:35, "By this everyone will know that you are my disciples, if you love one another." As believers, we walk by faith and we walk in love, just as the Colossians did. Walking by faith makes us strong, and loving people makes us happy.

As I noted in the introduction to this book, many scholars believe Epaphras is the person who wrote to Paul in prison and told him about the heresy of Gnosticism that was confusing the believers in Colossae. Colossians 1:4–8 shows us that not only did Epaphras report that problem to Paul, but he also made a point to share with him that the Colossians were full of love in the Spirit. Good ministers and leaders recognize and highlight the positive even when they have a problem they need to deal with. Just telling people what is wrong with the world or what they are doing wrong can be defeating, but if we also share the things that are good and right, it enables people to deal with the problem without being overwhelmed by it.

Faith and Love Based on Hope

According to Colossians 1:5, the Colossian believers had great faith and love because they had hope. Hope is simply an expectation that something good is about to happen to you at any minute, and it is the foundation of faith. There are people who believe faith is all they need. But if they say they have faith and also have a negative attitude and don't truly believe that anything good will happen, then they do not really have faith because hope is what faith stands on.

Because hope is so powerful, the enemy tries to steal it. I urge you not to let him do that, because if he cannot take away your hope, then his operations against you are compromised. No matter what happens, keep saying and believing that something good is going to happen for you. Maybe it didn't happen yesterday, maybe it didn't happen today, but it may happen in the next five minutes. If it doesn't happen tonight, it may happen tomorrow. If you can keep your hope strong, you can keep your faith strong, too.

Isaiah 40:31 helps us understand this. Many people are familiar with this in the King James Version, which says, "But they that wait upon the LORD shall renew their strength; they shall mount up with wings as eagles; they shall run, and not be weary; and they shall walk, and not faint." Do you know what the word *wait* means? It doesn't mean to go sit in a chair somewhere and do nothing until God moves. The word *wait* has the same definition as the word *hope*. In fact, the NIV uses *hope* instead of *wait* in this verse, and the Amplified Bible explains that those who wait on the Lord are those "who expect, look for, and hope in Him" (AMP). So to wait means to wait expectantly, looking and longing for God to move in your life. If you are not waiting with expectation, then you are not waiting according to what the Bible means when it talks about waiting on God. One of the best things you can do for yourself is to learn to wait hopefully.

You can get up every day, excited to see what God is going to do. You never know what He may do at any given moment in your life, and I believe most people need to expect more than they are expecting. I'm expecting something great to happen today. I don't know what it's going to be, but I'm expectant. You may ask, "What if nothing happens?" Then I'm going to expect something good to happen on the way home or when I get home or in the middle of the night. You can raise your joy to a whole new level all by yourself by simply living in expectation. You don't have to have any music. You don't have to have anyone preaching to you. All you need to do is get full of hope. I encourage you to say every morning, "Something good is going to happen to me today." That declaration will get your day off to a positive start.

The apostle Peter writes that when we are born again, we are born again into "an ever-living hope" (1 Pet. 1:3 AMP). Don't ever let the devil steal your hope. Every promise in the Bible is for you, and I urge you to take each one personally.

Personal Reflection

What are some things you are waiting for God to do with an expectation that it will happen at any time?

_____

_____

_____

_____

_____

_____

CHAPTER 4

A POWERFUL APOSTOLIC PRAYER

The Purpose of Paul's Prayer

In several of his epistles, Paul includes an apostolic prayer for those who read his letters. You can find one here, in Colossians 1:9–12, and also in Ephesians 1:17–19 and 3:16–19, and in Philippians 1:9–11, among other places. Each one is phenomenal in its own way, and this one is no exception.

These prayers caught my attention one day years ago when I was praying—at least I was praying my version of what I thought prayer was at that time. Back then, I thought effective prayer had to be long and loud and very spiritual-sounding. I did not know we could talk with God just as we talk with people, in normal tones about ordinary issues. I felt fairly certain that my husband, Dave, never prayed because when he said he was praying, he was simply sitting and looking out the window with his eyes open. I thought, *That's not prayer. You have to close your eyes if you are going to pray.* That is one of many common but silly religious ideas people get about prayer. Prayer is not answered because we get on our knees or use eloquent speech or because our eyes are open or shut. Prayer is answered because of our faith in God and because of His goodness.

God challenged me to compare my prayers to the prayers Jesus prayed and the prayers Paul prayed. That instruction felt a bit like a homework assignment, and I wanted to be obedient to do it, so I went through my Bible looking for examples of Jesus' prayers and of Paul's. As I studied Paul's prayers, not one time could I find that Paul asked God to remove people's problems. Instead, he prayed that God would empower them to endure whatever they had to face and to keep a good attitude in the midst of it.

Most of us would not be happy if we were going through difficult times and our spiritual leaders would not pray for our problems to go away. No one would like it if I said to them, "I'm not going to pray for your problems to go away. No, I'm not praying for that. But I will pray for you to get through them and that you will keep your faith strong and continue to love others." People would probably say, "No, thanks. I don't really want that prayer. I want to be free from my problem." Paul did not pray that way.

Nor did Paul pray about anything he had to have in order to stay saved. I think you know what I mean. "God, if You don't do this one thing, I am just not sure I can go on as a Christian. God, I don't think I can keep my faith unless You come through for me in this situation. I don't think I can hold on much longer if You don't do something." Instead of addressing physical problems, Paul prayed for spiritual growth and strength and for other spiritual blessings that would help the believers much more than they would have been helped had God removed their difficult circumstances.

For this reason, since the day we heard about you, we have not stopped praying for you. We continually ask

God to fill you with the knowledge of his will through all the wisdom and understanding that the Spirit gives, so that you may live a life worthy of the Lord and please him in every way: bearing fruit in every good work, growing in the knowledge of God, being strengthened with all power according to his glorious might so that you may have great endurance and patience, and giving joyful thanks to the Father, who has qualified you to share in the inheritance of his holy people in the kingdom of light.

Colossians 1:9–12

This passage of Scripture is a powerful prayer to pray for yourself and for the people you love. I encourage you to read it again and think about what it would mean in your life and in the lives of the people around you for you to be praying these things regularly and to experience God's answers.

Let's look at each verse of this passage individually.

A Prayer to Know God's Will

Colossians 1:9

For this reason, since the day we heard about you, we have not stopped praying for you. We continually ask God to fill you with the knowledge of his will through all the wisdom and understanding that the Spirit gives.

To summarize this first verse of Paul's prayer, he is simply praying that we would know the will of God in a deep way, that we would have discernment to see beyond the surface of things, and that we would truly know what it means to walk in and be led and guided by the Spirit.

Personal Reflection

Are you praying for yourself and for those you love to know God's will and walk in it? What are you doing to walk in God's will for your life as you currently understand it?

A Prayer to Please God, Bear Fruit, and Grow Spiritually

Colossians 1:10

So that you may live a life worthy of the Lord and please him in every way: bearing fruit in every good work, growing in the knowledge of God.

Paul wanted the early Christians to go deeper in their faith. That's part of what you are doing for yourself as you read this book; it's helping the roots of your faith go deeper in God. The Amplified Bible renders the last part of Colossians 1:10 this way: "bearing fruit in every good work and steadily growing in the knowledge of God [with deeper faith, clearer insight and fervent love for His precepts]." The way to go deeper is to steadily grow in your personal knowledge of God. I don't mean only knowledge *about* God, but personal experience of His faithfulness and love for you. This will strengthen your faith, increase your spiritual insight, and cause your love for Him to become more fervent.

One way we grow in our relationship with God is to mature in prayer. What if we were to pray each morning, "God, I want to please You today. Help me walk in Your will and be a blessing to others"? But we usually approach God with a list of things we want Him to do for us. "God, You've got to change my spouse. God, I need that promotion at work. God, I need a bigger house"—and on and on. But as we grow spiritually, our prayers change. Studying the prayers of Jesus and the prayers of Paul helped me see how self-centered my prayers were, and I felt God challenge me not to ask for one more "thing" until He released me to do so. It was like fasting from selfish, carnal prayers.

For six months, I did not feel I could ask God for anything materialistic. All I could say was, "God, I need more of You." Of course, various requests would come to mind and sometimes come out of my mouth. When they did, I simply said, "Never mind, God. I just need more of You."

The reason asking for more of God is so important is that everything we need is found in Him. We are complete in Him (Col. 2:10). In Him we have everything we need to live a godly life (2 Pet. 1:3). Our peace is in Him, our joy is in Him, and our strength is in Him.

This does not mean we do not or cannot desire other things, things the world offers or things that meet our practical needs. But God wants us to keep Him first, to hunger for Him above all else, and to be completely satisfied with Him. God was teaching me this lesson, and it was an important one that marked a good change in my walk with God. If we put Him first, He will add all the other things we need (Matt. 6:33).

Personal Reflection

In what ways could your prayer life change for the better?

_____

_____

_____

_____

_____

_____

_____

A Prayer for Endurance, Patience, and Stability

Colossians 1:11

Being strengthened with all power according to his glorious might so that you may have great endurance and patience.

When I think of people who are strengthened with God's power and who have great endurance and patience, the word that comes to mind is *stable*. These people are not emotionally up and down depending on what is happening in their lives; they aren't high one day and low the next because of the situations they face. They are strong, and they can persevere steadily through life's ups and downs. Although they may be hurting, their relationship with God helps them trust Him to heal them while they continue helping others and fulfilling their daily responsibilities.

A great prayer to pray for ourselves is, "God, help me be stable. I don't want to be emotionally up one day and down the next depending on what my circumstances are. I want to be stable and steady. I want to be a person whom others can depend on to be the same, no matter what is going on. I want my relationship with You to be stable. I want to love and trust You when I feel I'm on a mountaintop and when I feel I'm in a valley. I want to be willing to obey You whether You call me to do something I will enjoy or when You ask me to do something I won't like at all. I want to live with steadfastness and stability in my heart and mind, in my personality, in my relationships with others, and in my walk with You."

Nothing will exhaust a person like long-term emotional ups and downs. If you have struggled with them and had enough, let me encourage you to begin to pray all of Paul's apostolic prayer in Colossians 1, especially verse 11.

Give Joyful Thanks

Colossians 1:12

And giving joyful thanks to the Father, who has qualified you to share in the inheritance of his holy people in the kingdom of light.

Being thankful is the answer to many of our bad moods. Always thank God for what you do have more than you complain about what you do not have. Gratitude releases joy and enables you to give what Paul refers to as "joyful thanks."

CHAPTER 5

—◦—

WHAT WE HAVE IN CHRIST

Rescued from Sin, Brought into God's Kingdom

Colossians 1:13–14

For he has rescued us from the dominion of darkness and brought us into the kingdom of the Son he loves, in whom we have redemption, the forgiveness of sins.

Colossians 1:13–14 is another passage we can understand more thoroughly if we read it in the Amplified Bible, Classic Edition: "[The Father] has delivered *and* drawn us to Himself out of the control *and* the dominion of darkness and has transferred us into the kingdom of the Son of His love, in whom we have our redemption *through His blood*, [which means] the forgiveness of our sins."

Notice that Colossians 1:13 is in the past tense. It does not say that God *will* rescue us or deliver and draw us, but that He has already done so. Spiritually speaking, He has already brought us out of darkness. In Christ, God has accomplished many spiritual realities for us.

Spiritual realities are legally achieved in the heavenly realm, but if we don't feel the effect in our natural lives, we question whether they have been enacted. When we question, we begin to pray for circumstances we've already been granted. Part of spiritual maturity is learning to accept and receive what God has done for us instead of continually asking for what He has already said in His Word belongs to us. Remember, Hebrews 11:1 teaches us that faith is the title deed to all that is ours in Christ. Even if we do not yet see it or have not yet experienced it, it still belongs to us—not because we deserve it, but because God has provided it to us by His grace.

We have been given many gifts in Christ, and I want to focus on several of them now.

Wisdom

Wisdom helps us know what to do and how to make good decisions, and we need it in every area of our lives. Paul writes in 1 Corinthians 1:30: "It is because of him that you are in Christ Jesus, who has become for us wisdom from God—that is, our righteousness, holiness and redemption." Instead of praying, "God, I just need wisdom," we can say, "God, I thank You that because I am in Christ, I have wisdom, and I ask You to help me walk in it."

Peace

We don't need to pray for peace, saying, "Oh, God, I am just not at peace. Give me peace, Lord. Please give me peace." In Paul's letter to the Ephesians, he explains that Jesus Himself "is our peace" (Eph. 2:14). He writes in Romans 5:1, "Therefore, since we have been justified through faith, we have peace with God." When we know Jesus, we have peace. Jesus personally says in John 14:27, "Peace I leave with you; my peace I give you. I do not give to you as the world gives. Do not let your hearts be troubled and do not be afraid." In the Amplified Bible, Classic Edition, Jesus says, "*My [own] peace* I now give *and* bequeath to you" (emphasis mine). Jesus has given us the same quality of peace that He has. We do not have to ask God for peace or fear that we will not have it. We can simply say, "Thank You, God, for giving me peace. Now give me the grace to walk in peace and stop allowing myself to get upset, anxious, or fearful."

Authority and Power

In Luke 10:19, Jesus says, "Behold! I have given you authority *and* power to trample upon serpents and scorpions, and [physical and mental strength and ability] over all the power that the enemy [possesses]; and nothing shall in any way harm you" (AMPC). Notice that this statement, too, is in the past tense. He does not say, "I will give you power and authority," but "I *have given*" it to you. Just think about how different your life would be if you would believe and say, "I have power. I have authority." These promises and others like them are good ones to declare or speak aloud. This helps remind you of what is already yours in Christ.

Luke 10:19 does not say that nothing will come against us; however, it indicates that nothing has the ability to permanently harm us. It's important to realize that while the enemy does have power, he does not have authority. Jesus stripped him of his authority at the cross (Col. 2:14–15). When he does have authority over us, it is usually because we have given it to him through unbelief. We have God-given authority and power over the enemy, and we are victorious in Christ. We need to stop thinking thoughts of weakness and start thinking thoughts of strength and power. We are weak in ourselves, but we are powerful in Christ. Remember Philippians 4:13, which says, "I can do all things through Christ who strengthens me" (NKJV).

God's Love

Everyone wants to be loved, and thank God, we can be confident that He loves us unconditionally. He said through the prophet Jeremiah, "I have loved you with an everlasting love; I have drawn you with unfailing kindness" (Jer. 31:3). The well-known verse John 3:16 says, "For God so loved the world that he gave his one and only Son, that whoever believes in him shall not perish but have eternal life." If we are in the world, as all of us are, we can count on the fact that God loves us.

Receiving God's unconditional love personally is the foundation for our faith. How can we put our faith in someone unless we have assurance that they love us? Not only does God love us, but His love allows us to love Him in return and to love other people.

The Fruit of the Holy Spirit

In addition to what I have listed already, when we are in Christ, we also have the Holy Spirit. This means that all of the fruit of the Spirit is in us: love, joy, peace, forbearance, kindness, goodness, faithfulness, gentleness and self-control (Gal. 5:22–23).

I could fill an entire book with what we have "in Christ" and who we are in Him if we truly believe in Him and trust Him for the forgiveness of our sins. Sadly, like me, you may have been taught more about what you should *do* than you have been taught about *who you are* in Him. We have a new nature (2 Cor. 5:17), and it is important for us to learn to identify with our new identity. You are "in Christ," and He has loaded you down with benefits. Believe these things are yours, and soon you will see them grow in your life.

Personal Reflection

What do you believe about yourself? Are you in agreement with God, or are you still letting the world and the devil determine your worth and value? If so, what is one practical step you can take to begin making progress in this area?

_____

_____

_____

_____

_____

_____

_____

Righteousness (Right Standing with God)

Paul writes in 2 Corinthians 5:21 that God made Jesus "to be sin for us, so that *in him we might become the righteousness of God*" (emphasis mine). We don't need to beg God to make us righteous. We can thank Him that He *has made us righteous* in Christ.

I sometimes hear about people who feel God is angry with them and who view the problems in their lives as punishment from Him. This saddens me, because it is simply not true. Yet I understand it, because for many years one question went through my head: "What's wrong with me?" And every time I made a mistake, I thought God was angry with me. My earthly father was always angry about one thing or another, and I usually assumed I had done something wrong, so I carried that thinking over into my relationship with God. But God is nothing like ordinary people, nor does He behave the way they do.

Please understand: God is not looking to punish us; Jesus took our punishment through His death on the cross. All the punishment we would ever deserve for all the sins we would ever commit was placed on Jesus when He died for us. When we sin, all we need to do is repent and receive the forgiveness that is already ours. (I will elaborate on this in the next section.)

God does not want us to be afraid He will punish us. The devil wants us to feel that way—to live in fear and to be miserable. I want to make sure you know that you are not wrong with God; you are made right with God through the blood of Jesus Christ.

Being right with God through Christ does not mean you do everything right all the time. No one does. But there is a difference between your *who* and your *do*. *Who we are* in Christ and *what we do* as flawed human beings are two different things. When we first come to Christ, we don't know this truth and usually carry old thinking into our new life in Christ. But thankfully, as we learn the truth of God's Word and act on it, it makes us free.

We grow from being baby Christians to being fully formed into Christ's image. 2 Corinthians 3:18 tells us: "And we all, with unveiled face, *continually* seeing as in a mirror the glory of the Lord, are *progressively* being transformed into His image from [one degree of] glory to [even more] glory, which comes from the Lord, [who is] the Spirit" (AMP). This idea of going "from glory to glory" means that we continually move closer and closer to who He wants us to be.

Going from glory to glory means that you are changing and growing every day as you walk with God. A good example I use in my teaching is that of a little boy trying to wear his dad's coat. He is so proud of it, and he actually thinks it looks really good, but the coat is way too big for him. Let's say his dad tells him he can keep it. He gets very excited, I am sure, but he has to patiently grow into the coat. Every time he puts it on to see how it looks, it fits him a tiny bit better. As he continues to grow, the coat will one day be a perfect fit. Using that word picture, now consider all that is yours in Christ. You have it; it is yours—but you may not feel you fit into all of it perfectly just yet.

If you are the type of person who becomes angry or frustrated with yourself every time you do something wrong, I hope you will stop that. Realize instead that if you love God and you have received Jesus as your Savior, you probably aren't where you need to be in your thoughts, words, and actions. But you aren't where you used to be, either—you are growing! Your relationship with God is a journey, not a one-time event.

Personal Reflection

How have you changed and matured since you first became a believer?

_____

_____

_____

_____

_____

_____

Forgiveness of Sin

Notice that Colossians 1:14 says that in Christ, "we have redemption, the forgiveness of sins." It's not something we have to "get" from God. It's something we receive. We often try to "get" things God has already given, and to *get* means "to obtain by struggle and effort." To *receive*, though, means "to take in what is being offered." God's forgiveness of sin is something we receive. It is a free gift from God.

Jesus has already paid for all of our sins. His death on the cross is a finished work. He died a painful death in our place for every sin we have ever committed or ever will commit. And He did it so we could be in intimate relationship with God through Him. Because of His death on the cross, sin has been thoroughly dealt with. All we need to do is believe and receive that truth. The Bible says we are "dead to sin but alive to God in Christ Jesus" (Rom. 6:11). We do not always feel that we are dead to sin, but as we continue to believe what God says instead of how we feel, our feelings will come in line with the truth of God's Word.

Paul states in Romans 6:2, "We are those who have died to sin," and asks, "how can we live in it any longer?" The more we believe we are dead to sin, the more we will realize that there is a part of us that wants nothing to do with sin. Sometimes we feel tempted to sin, and we fight within ourselves, trying not to give in to the temptation when all we need to do is say, "I am dead to sin. The real me—the born-again me—does not even want to be jealous or greedy or anything else God does not approve of. So, flesh, listen to me: You are not going to get your way. God has given me the power to resist temptation, and, through the power of the Holy Spirit, I will not sin." To live in the reality of being dead to sin, we must first believe that we are dead to it and then enforce that belief with our thoughts, words, and actions.

In a way, the apostle John answers Paul's question about how we cannot live in sin in 1 John 3:9. He indicates that a truly born-again person cannot live a life of sin. "No one who is born of God [deliberately, knowingly, and habitually] practices sin, because God's seed...remains [permanently] in him...and he [who is born again] cannot *habitually* [live a life characterized by] sin, because he is born of God *and* longs to please Him" (AMP). Notice that this verse does not say a person who is born again *never* sins. We all sin and make mistakes (Rom. 3:23). This verse says a born-again believer does not "deliberately, knowingly, and habitually" sin. Why? Because when we are born of God, His nature abides in us and we long to please Him.

Even though we sin and we know our sins are forgiven, we still need to be repentant, and that means we are willing to turn completely away from sin. We may need to talk to God about our struggles with certain sins. This is not because He is unaware of our sin or because He has not already taken care of it, but because we need to get it out of our souls. We need to take responsibility for what we have done and for any sinful thoughts, words, or deeds. But we do not have to beg and plead for forgiveness. We simply need to say, "God, I admit that I did this. I don't want to continue to do it. I choose to turn away from sin. I am sorry for my sin, and I receive the forgiveness Jesus purchased for me on the cross." Forgiveness has been extended to us. It is a gift God has already provided. We simply need to receive it with thanksgiving.

Romans 6:4 says, "We were therefore buried with him through baptism into death in order that, just as Christ was raised from the dead...we too may live a new life." We are new in Christ (2 Cor. 5:17). The past is gone. God's mercies are new for us every morning (Lam. 3:22-23), and every one of us has a new life to live each day.

The forgiveness of sin and everything I have mentioned in this section—wisdom, peace, authority and power, righteousness, God's love, and the fruit of the Holy Spirit—are part of what Colossians 1:13 means when it says God has "rescued us from the dominion of darkness and brought us into the kingdom of the Son he loves" because all of these amazing blessings are part of His kingdom.

CHAPTER 6

WHO JESUS IS

The Image of God

Colossians 1:15–17

The Son is the image of the invisible God, the firstborn
over all creation. For in him all things were created: things
in heaven and on earth, visible and invisible, whether
thrones or powers or rulers or authorities; all things have
been created through him and for him. He is before all
things, and in him all things hold together.

We know that Jesus is the image of God, meaning that He shows us exactly who God is. God is Spirit, and we cannot see Him (John 4:24). But Jesus came to earth as a person who could be seen and who could walk, talk, eat, feel emotion, and understand other human beings (John 1:14). He was fully man and fully God at the same time. As the image of God, He represented God accurately.

Paul writes in 2 Corinthians 4:4 that "the god of this age has blinded the minds of unbelievers, so that they cannot see the light of the gospel that displays the glory of Christ, *who is the image of God*" (emphasis mine). And Hebrews 1:3 refers to Jesus as "the brightness" of God's glory and "the express image of His person" (NKJV).

Perhaps the passage that most reminds us of Colossians

1:15–17 and helps us understand it is John 1:1–5, in which Jesus is called "the Word":

> In the beginning was the Word, and the Word was with God, and the Word was God. He was with God in the beginning. Through him all things were made; without him nothing was made that has been made. In him was life, and that life was the light of all mankind. The light shines in the darkness, and the darkness has not overcome it.

Although there was a specific time when Jesus came to earth, He existed with God before He was made manifest in His earthly body, which is why Paul calls Him "the firstborn over all creation" and says that "in him all things were created."

The Supremacy and Headship of Christ

Colossians 1:18

*And he is the head of the body, the church; he is the
beginning and the firstborn from among the dead, so that
in everything he might have the supremacy.*

As I mentioned in the introduction to this book, the theme
of Paul's letter to the Colossians is the headship of Christ.
He is over and above everything. He is the head, and we are
the body (Eph. 1:22–23). He is in control, and we are to follow His instructions and example. As long as the body takes
direction from the head, we will be in good shape. But when
the body starts trying to be in control, that's when things
become disorderly, confusing, and out of balance.

Even though Christ is the head and we look to Him to
know what to do, this does not mean that believers have no
responsibility or free will. God always allows us to choose
whether or not we will follow Him. If we do, we have certain
responsibilities. Our primary responsibility is to mature spiritually and represent God by really living out the resurrection
life Jesus offers us.

Paul writes about the resurrection life in Philippians 3:10,
when he talks about knowing Christ and "the power of his
resurrection." That means you can be right here on earth,

going to work, going home, doing the dishes, cutting the grass, going through everything that everyone else experiences and still live in the power of Jesus' resurrection. The resurrection life available to Christians does not guarantee you will never have problems; it simply offers us a place in Christ to rise above the storms of life because we know that Christ is our head and He is in control of everything.

If we do not relate to Jesus as our head—if we do not give Him first place in our lives—then whatever we do put in first place will be an idol to us. The apostle John writes, "Dear children, keep yourselves from idols" (1 John 5:21). All sorts of things try to become idols, meaning they will fight for first place in our lives. Many of these will be things that are considered "good," such as family, working hard, friends, or even serving God in ministry.

I urge you to guard against any sort of substitute that would try to supersede Him and take first place in your life. Do you know that it's possible for anything to become an idol in our lives, even the things you'd never expect? There was a time in my life, many years ago, when the ministry I was trying to build—the ministry God gave me—became more important to me than God. I did not mean for that to happen, but it did. It can happen to anyone. I was so proud of myself because I was in ministry, working for God and serving on the staff of a well-known church in St. Louis. When I looked at my life, I thought I was doing so well. But one day the Lord spoke clearly to my heart: "You are proud of yourself because you are working *for* Me. The problem is that you are not spending any time *with* Me." That was an important lesson for me to learn, and I have never forgotten it.

I want to take a moment to encourage those who work in full-time ministry: Be careful; be alert and diligent not to allow the growth or popularity of your ministry to become more important to you than God. I spend personal time with God every morning before I even think about trying to get a message to give to someone else. I focus on the things that are going on between God and me, because it is useless for me to teach a biblical message to an audience if I am ignoring God in my personal life or not listening to what He is saying to me.

Whether you serve in ministry or not, nothing is more important than your relationship with God. Keep Him first in all things, and everything else will fall into its proper place.

When we put Jesus first, we acknowledge that He is the head and we are part of the body, and we surrender everything about ourselves to Him. This idea makes some people nervous, because they are afraid that if they put Jesus first, they may have to give up something that really means a lot to them. The psalmist David writes about this in Psalm 37:4: "Take delight in the Lord, and he will give you the desires of your heart." I can personally assure you: If you put Jesus first, you will be amazed at how much God will do for you. His joy and peace will fill your heart, and you will receive the desires of your heart in God's perfect timing. This doesn't mean you won't have challenges, but you will be able to overcome them by the power of the Holy Spirit and live your life by His grace.

Personal Reflection

Have you surrendered everything to God, giving Him first place in your life? If not, what do you need to surrender? How can you make God your number-one priority in every area of your life—your time, thoughts, relationships, work, hobbies, and elsewhere?

_____

_____

_____

_____

_____

_____

_____

Jesus Our Reconciler

Colossians 1:19–23

For God was pleased to have all his fullness dwell in him, and through him to reconcile to himself all things, whether things on earth or things in heaven, by making peace through his blood, shed on the cross. Once you were alienated from God and were enemies in your minds because of your evil behavior. But now he has reconciled you by Christ's physical body through death to present you holy in his sight, without blemish and free from accusation—if you continue in your faith, established and firm, and do not move from the hope held out in the gospel. This is the gospel that you heard and that has been proclaimed to every creature under heaven, and of which I, Paul, have become a servant.

Before Adam and Eve sinned in the garden (Gen. 3:6), God had a plan to reconcile everything back to Himself—a plan to restore fellowship between humanity and Himself and bring all things back into balance. The devil will not succeed in thwarting God's plan, because it has already been completed in Christ. Everyone is not living in its fullness, but it is a finished work. Prayerfully, everyone is on the way to experiencing and displaying completeness in Him.

To reconcile is to restore friendly relations between two parties. It means to cause people to live in harmony. It is a beautiful thought that Christ has restored friendly relations between us and Father God.

Sin separates us from God, but Christ accomplished the work of reconciling us to Him through His death on the cross. Peter writes: "For you know that it was not with perishable things such as silver or gold that you were redeemed from the empty way of life handed down to you from your ancestors, *but with the precious blood of Christ*" (1 Pet. 1:18–19, emphasis mine).

When Jesus poured out His blood on the cross and suffered in agony, He did it to buy us back from the devil, who alienated us from God and wants to keep us alienated from Him. As believers, we belong to God. We don't belong to the world or to the enemy. We are reconciled to God through Christ. We are in right relationship with Him through Christ. And we are "holy in His sight."

Personal Reflection

How has Jesus made it possible for you to be in right relationship with God?

_____

_____

_____

_____

_____

_____

_____

Rejoicing in Suffering, Hoping in Christ

Colossians 1:24–26

*Now I rejoice in what I am suffering for you, and I fill
up in my flesh what is still lacking in regard to Christ's
afflictions, for the sake of his body, which is the church. I
have become its servant by the commission God gave me to
present to you the word of God in its fullness—the mystery
that has been kept hidden for ages and generations, but is
now disclosed to the Lord's people.*

Perhaps better than anyone else who wrote any of the books
of the Bible, Paul knew how to rejoice in suffering. He writes
about his suffering in 2 Corinthians 11, when he is talking
about false apostles:

I have worked much harder, been in prison more fre-
quently, been flogged more severely, and been exposed
to death again and again. Five times I received from the
Jews the forty lashes minus one. Three times I was beaten
with rods, once I was pelted with stones, three times I was
shipwrecked…I have been in danger from rivers, in danger from bandits, in danger from my fellow Jews, in danger
from Gentiles; in danger in the city, in danger in the coun-
try, in danger at sea; and in danger from false believers.

I have labored and toiled and have often gone without sleep; I have known hunger and thirst and have often gone without food; I have been cold and naked.

2 Corinthians 11:23–27

Obviously, Paul was acquainted with suffering. He can urge us to rejoice in our sufferings because he learned to rejoice in his. We don't rejoice because we are suffering; no one enjoys suffering. But we rejoice that we have hope through Christ in the midst of our struggles. He elaborates on the value of rejoicing when we suffer in Romans 5:3–4: "We also glory in our sufferings, because we know that suffering produces perseverance; perseverance, character; and character, hope."

The apostle James also teaches us about the positive aspects of suffering as believers: "Consider it pure joy, my brothers and sisters, whenever you face trials of many kinds, because you know that the testing of your faith produces perseverance" (James 1:2–3). For most of us, our first response to trials or suffering is not joy. We may be tempted to complain, or to become angry, or to grow fearful. That would be the natural way to respond, but Christians can respond differently because we know that God is on our side and that He is our vindicator.

James says to rejoice in trials because they produce perseverance. But they can produce a lot of other things before perseverance shows itself strong. They can pull us into self-pity, pride, fear, rebellion, selfishness, jealousy, and other negative conditions. But we don't need to allow negative emotions to boss us around and tell us what to do. We can learn to feel the feelings but not let them control how we behave.

Part of our Christian walk involves being conformed to the image of Christ (Rom. 8:29), and that is a journey that isn't always easy. As we go through that lifelong process, we will face challenges and suffering as Christ, Paul, and others have faced. God does not allow suffering in our lives simply so we will suffer and learn to be tough. He uses it to strengthen us in our relationship with Him and to bring forth godly character qualities that may not be formed in us any other way. And when we learn how to remain stable in the midst of the storms of life, it is a great witness to unbelievers.

Personal Reflection

How has God used suffering to strengthen you and draw you closer to Him?

_____

_____

_____

_____

_____

_____

Christ in You, the Hope of Glory

Colossians 1:27

To them God has chosen to make known among the
Gentiles the glorious riches of this mystery, which is Christ
in you, the hope of glory.

Colossians 1:27 is one of the most amazing verses in the New Testament, but we may read it and wonder what it means. The word *glory* means the manifestation of all the excellencies of God. We cannot be glorified without Christ living in us, helping us every moment to be what He desires. On the other hand, we are His only hope of glory here on earth because He works through us. One of the ways He shows His power and greatness is in how He changes people after they receive Him as their Savior and Lord.

Jesus came to live in your heart through the Holy Spirit when you believed in and received Him. This means that you are His home. You are never left alone. You never have to do anything alone. You are never far away from the help or the hope you need. God is never more than one thought away from you. The moment you turn your thoughts toward Him, you become aware of how near He is to you.

You may be thinking, *Well, that is a nice Scripture, but I don't act very glorious much of the time.*

Let me use a biological example to explain this further. When a man and a woman have a sexual relationship and the husband's seed is planted in his wife's womb, she becomes pregnant with his child. When Christ comes to live in a believer's heart, we become pregnant, so to speak, with everything God is. Jesus is called the "Seed" (Gen. 3:15) and the "seed" of everything God is and has is in us.

You may be pregnant with all kinds of spiritual things, but you have not given birth to them yet. You may even be feeling the birth pains of labor. Paul writes, "My dear children, for whom I am again in the pains of childbirth until Christ is formed in you" (Gal. 4:19). Paul deeply desired for the believers to be fully formed into the image of Christ. He wanted to present them spiritually mature. We want that also, and like Paul, sometimes we feel the pangs of labor as we allow God to bring forth something new in our lives.

When a woman is pregnant, she believes she will hold her baby in her arms when she delivers. The baby is alive in her but has not yet come forth into the world where she can see it, hear it, hold it, and talk to it. She knows she will have to endure a time of waiting and preparation. The same is true spiritually. As a believer, seeds have been planted in you— seeds of goodness, seeds of love, seeds of peace, seeds of joy, seeds of righteousness, and others—but they will not burst into a harvest overnight. In time, as you continue to walk with God and in obedience to Him, and as you grow in your knowledge of Him, the seeds will develop into good fruit in your behavior that will please God and draw others to Him.

We must learn to be patient, because being fully formed into the image of Christ is a process. Even after we are made new creatures in Christ and have new desires, we also struggle with old desires. Sometimes this makes us feel very confused. Paul understood this struggle and wrote about it in Romans 7:15–20: "I do not understand what I do. For what I want to do I do not do, but what I hate I do . . . For I do not do the good I want to do, but the evil I do not want to do—this I keep on doing. Now if I do what I do not want to do, it is no longer I who do it, but it is sin living in me that does it."

The enemy uses our old desires and old habits to tempt us to sin. He wants us to become discouraged and question our salvation. He wants us to forget that we are new creatures in Christ and that God's nature abides in us. His goal is to entice us to think, *Well, nothing happened to me when I said I got saved. I'm no different than I used to be. How can I act like this and say I am a Christian?* When thoughts like these come, we need to respond by saying, "Jesus is living in me, and I'm a new creation in Him."

You already have everything you need inside of you. You simply need to believe it. You don't have to wear yourself out fighting bad behavior. All you need to do is remember who you are in Christ. Continue studying God's Word and spend time with Him. Using self-control and choosing to do the right thing instead of the wrong thing you are being tempted to do isn't difficult if you are deeply rooted in God's love for you and the knowledge of who you are in Him. If you are steadfast and diligent, you will experience progress, little by little, as you become more like Christ every day.

Personal Reflection

What will you tell the enemy the next time he reminds you of all your faults?

_____

_____

_____

_____

_____

_____

_____

Trying to "be good" on your own without abiding in Christ will only frustrate you, so decide instead to receive the grace God extends to you and let Him do the work of changing you into the person He has given you the ability to be. No amount of human effort to change yourself will be effective unless you go to God and say, "I really want to live better, but nothing I try will work without You. I know You have put good things in me, but I need You to bring them out of me. Help me, Lord, to give birth to all the good things in me."

The process of manifesting who we are in Christ does not come quickly or without opposition because the devil continues to lie to us. It is important to remember that anything that does not agree with God's Word is a lie, and until we stop believing lies, we won't see the changes we desire.

I have learned many things, and I am still learning and still uncovering lies the devil has used to deceive me. If you find yourself frustrated along the journey of spiritual growth, just remember not to turn against yourself, not to live with guilt or regret or feeling condemned, wondering what is wrong with you because you can't do everything right. We all make mistakes. You do not have to compare your spiritual growth to anyone else's. All you need to do is to believe the Word of God, stay in fellowship with Jesus, and keep on keeping on. The more you keep going forward and refuse to quit, the more deeply rooted in Christ you will become. Every day you don't quit is a day you make progress.

The psalmist describes a deeply rooted person this way:

Blessed is the one who does not walk in step with the wicked or stand in the way that sinners take or sit in the company of mockers, but whose delight is in the law of the LORD, and who meditates on his law day and night. That person is like a tree planted by streams of water, which yields its fruit in season and whose leaf does not wither—whatever they do prospers.

Psalm 1:1–3

Notice that the person who is like a deeply rooted tree meditates on God's Word "day and night." To *meditate* on God's Word is to be like a cow chewing its cud—to chew on it and chew on it and chew on it. When you eat your food, chewing it well is important. If you don't, you will not get all the benefits of eating it. You can apply this idea to the way you approach God's Word. Meditating on the Word involves thinking about it in depth, rolling it over and over in your mind, asking the Holy Spirit to reveal its meaning, and pondering how you can apply it to your life. The word *meditate* actually means "to confess or to mutter over and over," almost under your breath. Confessing the Word helps you focus on it and helps it get established in your heart and mind.

The way to discover everything God has for you is to meditate on His Word and to hear and read it over and over again. It will teach you what it means to be in Christ and to know Him as the hope of glory.

CHAPTER 7

SPIRITUAL MATURITY AND KNOWING WHAT IS YOURS IN CHRIST

Three Keys to Spiritual Growth

Colossians 1:28–29

He is the one we proclaim, admonishing and teaching
everyone with all wisdom, so that we may present everyone
fully mature in Christ. To this end I strenuously contend
with all the energy Christ so powerfully works in me.

Paul concludes Colossians 1 by declaring that Christ is the one he proclaims—not himself, not anyone else, but Christ. He teaches wisely, with one goal in mind: to "present everyone fully mature in Christ." This should be the goal of anyone who teaches and preaches the Word of God. The goal should not be to make a congregation feel good all the time. Of course, leaders in the church are to encourage and build up people, to comfort them in times of difficulty, to recognize and call out the gifts of God in them, and to help them feel loved and accepted. But there are also times when a good leader will tell someone, "That attitude is not helping you as a Christian," or "Those actions are not representing Christ well." Our job is to present you to the Lord fully mature, as a full-grown believer who can be a great example in the world. Paul instructs Timothy to "correct, rebuke and encourage" those he taught (2 Tim. 4:2). Any spiritual leader who teaches the full counsel of God's Word will end up doing all of these and will help believers mature spiritually.

Each of us should also have spiritual maturity as one of our personal goals. There are many ways to grow in Christ, but I want to focus on just three of them here. All of them relate to the way you spend your time: time with God, time in God's Word, and time with the right people.

Time with God

There is nothing better than one-on-one time with God. During this time, you can read, study, pray, and talk with God, or simply sit in His presence and rest in Him. I once heard that people can be as close to God as they want to be; it all depends on how much time they are willing to put into their personal relationship with Him. Spending time with God is not a religious obligation; it is a rare and wonderful privilege.

Time in God's Word

I encourage you to invest a lot of time studying and meditating on God's Word. You are investing time by reading this book, and I believe it will help and strengthen you not just right now, but for weeks and months to come. Lessons and principles you are learning in this book will come back to you just when you need them in the future.

Investing time in God's Word as part of your everyday life is one of the best things you can do for your spiritual growth. In fact, it's an absolute necessity. The Word will guide you, encourage you, give you wisdom, and give you the confidence you need to face each day. Spending time in God's Word does not always mean reading the Bible. You can also read books that help explain the Bible or that offer teaching on a particular subject about which you are interested in learning more. You can also listen to podcasts, watch good sermons on television, or learn from various kinds of social media outlets.

Time with the Right People

If you really want to grow spiritually, you will need to spend time with people who can help you, people who are also hungry for the things of God. Make a priority of being around people who will build you up in your faith, not people who will try to pull you away from it. Think and pray about the types of people you need in your life as you walk with God, and ask God to bring them across your path and help you build godly relationships with them.

If you have friends who are tearing you down and bringing too much temptation into your life, you may find it necessary to separate from them for your own good.

Personal Reflection

In what ways can you increase the amount of time you spend with God, the time you spend in His Word, and the time you spend with the right people?

_____

_____

_____

_____

_____

_____

_____

Paul Contends for the Believers to Know Who They Are in Christ

Colossians 2:1–5

I want you to know how hard I am contending for you and for those at Laodicea, and for all who have not met me personally. My goal is that they may be encouraged in heart and united in love, so that they may have the full riches of complete understanding, in order that they may know the mystery of God, namely, Christ, in whom are hidden all the treasures of wisdom and knowledge. I tell you this so that no one may deceive you by fine-sounding arguments. For though I am absent from you in body, I am present with you in spirit and delight to see how disciplined you are and how firm your faith in Christ is.

In the second chapter of Colossians, Paul encourages his readers in several ways. He instructs us to keep learning, to continue to walk more and more deeply with God, to know who we are in Christ and what belongs to us in Him, and not to be deceived by philosophies or intellectual theories. All of these are important to our spiritual maturity.

Paul's opening words in Colossians 2 indicate the depth of his love and concern for the Christians at Colossae and also for those in Laodicea, a city approximately fifteen kilometers (about nine and a half miles) from Colossae. Apparently, the false teaching that threatened the Colossian church had spread to the believers in Laodicea, too. In this part of his letter, Paul continues to extend his care to those who have not met him personally, which shows us the strength of his commitment to believers in the early church. He clearly states his goal for all of them—to "be encouraged in heart and united in love," so they could know and understand Christ completely.

Notice how intense Paul's emotion is in this passage. He wrote that he was "contending" sincerely and passionately for those who would read his letter. In other words, he was fighting fervently for them. He was praying for them, and he was endeavoring to teach them all that he could about Christ. He understood the seriousness of the fact that false teachers sought to cause the early believers to stray from their faith, and he would not let them fall away without making his best effort to keep them close to the truths of the Christian faith. Paul had dealt with false teaching before, and he knew how dangerous it was. He had written to the Corinthians about five years before he wrote to the Colossians about this same issue, saying, "But I am afraid that just as Eve was deceived by the serpent's cunning, your minds may somehow be led astray from your sincere and pure devotion to Christ" (2 Cor. 11:3) or, as other versions render it, the "simplicity" that is in Christ.

Paul spent years ministering and writing so people could fully understand who Jesus is. He wanted them to be hungry to keep learning more and more, just as he was. I cannot think of a more worthy goal for any of us than to have a deep and personal knowledge and understanding of our Lord and Savior, Jesus Christ—not just knowing about Him, but *knowing* Him. Deception was rampant in Paul's day, but it is even more so in these times, and we need to always be prepared to combat it with the truth of God's Word.

Treasures Hidden in Christ

Notice what Paul writes about Jesus in Colossians 2:3. He says that in Christ "are hidden all the treasures of wisdom and knowledge." The treasures hidden in Him are endless, so no matter how spiritually mature a person may be or how long they have walked with Him, there is always more to learn and experience.

Whenever you need wisdom in a situation or anytime you need to know something, the answer is "hidden" in Christ. It is not hidden because God does not want you to find it; it is hidden because God wants you to seek it. He knows you will find the wisdom and knowledge you are diligently searching for, as well as other surprising and wonderful things. The process of seeking God offers many rewards—more than simply the immediate answers you may be looking for.

Discovering the treasures hidden in Christ is not difficult. You pray for the Holy Spirit to reveal them to you, and you take the time and effort to diligently study God's Word. You remain committed to God and His Word, no matter how long it takes to receive your answer.

Throughout Scripture, we read about valuable things that are hidden. For example, Jesus says in Matthew 13:44, "The kingdom of heaven is like treasure hidden in a field." The Bible also teaches us that hidden things are meant to be discovered. In Mark 4:22, Jesus says to a crowd listening to Him teach beside the Sea of Galilee, "For whatever is hidden is meant to be disclosed, and whatever is concealed is meant to be brought out into the open." One of the things God does is reveal to us what we cannot see with our natural eyes. Paul writes in 1 Corinthians 2:9–10: " 'What no eye has seen, what no ear has heard, and what no human mind has conceived'—the things that God has prepared for those who love him—these are the things God has revealed to us by his Spirit."

These verses should encourage you to search for all the treasures God has for you to discover and understand. While there will always be certain spiritual mysteries that are part of walking with God, He does not permanently hide from you anything you need to know. He may lead you on a journey to discover it through His Word, but if you seek it, you will find it. He promises in Jeremiah 29:13: "You will seek me and find me when you seek me with all your heart." Look at God's Word as though it is a treasure map that never stops revealing new treasures for you to enjoy.

Personal Reflection

What are some ways you can search for the treasures God has for you in His Word?

_____

_____

_____

_____

_____

_____

CHAPTER 8

KNOWING WHO YOU ARE IN CHRIST

Becoming the Person God Created You to Be

Colossians 2:6–7

So then, just as you received Christ Jesus as Lord,
continue to live your lives in him, rooted and built up in
him, strengthened in the faith as you were taught, and
overflowing with thankfulness.

Paul encourages the Colossians to continue to live in Christ in the same way that they received Him as Lord. They received Him as we do—by grace through faith (Eph. 2:8–9)—and we also live our lives in Him continually by faith. Remember that according to Colossians 1:4, faith is leaning "on Him with absolute confidence in His power, wisdom, and goodness" (AMP).

There are two little words in Colossians 2:6 that can change your life forever: *in him*, meaning *in Christ*. Paul has an amazing revelation on this subject and writes about it often. Later in this section I will list several places he writes about this in Colossians, but he writes about it in his other epistles, too. "Who we are in Christ" is our identity as believers. We do not have to let our own thoughts and opinions or those of other people define who we are. The Word of God tells us who we are in Him. Some people have had their identity stolen by the devil because they lacked knowledge of the truth, but it is not too late to overturn all the damage the devil has done.

When you became a believer, you began your journey in Christ. When you received Him as Savior, He came to live in your heart. Part of having Him in your heart means that you also have everything He offers you—love, acceptance, righteousness (right relationship with God), peace, joy, hope, victory over the enemy, forgiveness of sin, and other things. But all of these start as seeds. They are planted in you by Christ, and they simply need to grow. They grow as you grow in Christ. Just as a natural seed requires water in order to grow, spiritual seeds do, too. The way to water a spiritual seed is with the Word of God (Eph. 5:26). The way to become firmly established in your identity as a believer is to look up all the Scriptures that talk about being "in Him" and mark them in your Bible, study and meditate on them, and ask the Holy Spirit to cause them to take root in your heart and mind. You can also use the "Knowing Who I Am in Christ" list on our ministry website to discover more about all that is yours in Him. Visit joycemeyer.org/InChrist.

When we know who we are in Christ, our confidence is not based on what people think about us, whether we are invited to certain parties or events, whether we get the job we want, whether we are welcomed into social circles, whether we get a date with the person we have a crush on, or whether anything else happens in the circumstances of our lives. It's not that we don't want acceptance or enjoy those types of things. No one wants to feel disappointed or rejected. But when we know who we are in Christ, we can get through the challenges we face while remaining confident that our worth and value do not depend on any of them. Our significance is found in Christ alone.

If you learn what the Bible says about who you are in Christ and begin to study and meditate on these truths, even confessing them aloud over and over, it will change your life. You will understand who you really are, and that will change the way you see yourself, the way you relate to other people, your perspective of your future, and other important things.

I will list several Scriptures that show you who you are in Christ to give you an idea of how powerful they are. These are all from Colossians, so just imagine what you could learn if you were to study everything the Bible says about who you are in Christ. If you study and meditate on these truths, they will make an amazing difference in your life.

- I am strengthened with all power according to God's glorious might (Col. 1:11).
- I have been rescued from the dominion and the power of darkness and brought into God's kingdom (Col. 1:13).
- My life is rooted in my faith in Christ and I overflow with thanksgiving for all He has done for me (Col. 2:7).
- I am complete in Him Who is the head rule and authority over all—of every angelic and earthly power (Col. 2:10).
- I have been buried with Christ in baptism and raised with Him through faith (Col. 2:12).

- I have been made alive with Christ, and I have been forgiven of all my sins (Col. 2:13).
- I am renewed in the knowledge of God and no longer want to live in my old ways or nature before I accepted Christ (Col. 3:9–10).
- I am chosen and dearly loved by God (Col. 3:12).

Don't forget to check out the list of Scriptures on our website pertaining to who you are in Christ.

Personal Reflection

How are you living in the life-changing power of knowing who you are in Christ?

_____

_____

_____

_____

_____

_____

Rooted and Built Up in Him

Colossians 2:6–7

So then, just as you received Christ Jesus as Lord,
continue to live your lives in him, rooted and built up in
him, strengthened in the faith as you were taught, and
overflowing with thankfulness.

I want to continue looking at Colossians 2:6–7 and call your attention to Paul's comment in Colossians 2:7 about being "rooted and built up" in Christ. That is true in the natural world, and it is true in our spiritual lives. I like the way the Amplified Bible, Classic Edition renders Colossians 2:7 for several reasons. One reason is that it reads as an instruction: "Have the roots [of your being] firmly *and* deeply planted [in Him, fixed and founded in Him], being continually built up in Him, becoming increasingly more confirmed *and* established in the faith, just as you were taught, and abounding *and* overflowing in it with thanksgiving."

When Paul writes in Colossians 2:7 about "the roots of your being" he is referring to the depth of your inner life. We all have an inner life and an outward life. The outward life is what we present to other people. It may include the way we dress or style our hair, our behavior, the car we drive or the house we live in, our education, job, hobbies and interests, or our social networks and connections.

The inner life is what happens on the inside of us, where people cannot see it. It is its own world of thoughts, feelings, ideas, beliefs, and decisions. This is where our hearts are and where we connect with God. In fact, the Bible says: "For behold, the kingdom of God is within you [in your hearts]" (Luke 17:21 AMPC). A good life is not about what happens on the outside—our circumstances, or what people think of us, or how successful we seem to be by the world's standards. A good life is about what is going on inside of us.

I have learned that people can live under the best circumstances in the world but still be miserable if they have bad attitudes. If they think negatively or have negative emotions or do not like themselves, they will still be unhappy. On the other hand, people can face all kinds of challenges in their circumstances and still be joyful.

There are people in the world today facing financial trouble, family problems, health challenges, and all kinds of struggles, yet they know and trust the Lord, and they find joy and strength in Him. With the right mindset, a happy heart, a good attitude, and the confidence that God loves you, your inner life is strong, peaceful, and joyful. You can make it through life's tests and trials, and they don't even have to seem like major obstacles. They may still pose challenges for you, but they will not be made easier by a bad attitude, wrong thinking, or negative emotions.

Personal Reflection

How peaceful and joyful is your inner life? What can you do to grow stronger and be more stable during hard times?

_____

_____

_____

_____

_____

A second reason I appreciate the Amplified Bible, Classic Edition of this verse is that it emphasizes being rooted in Christ by saying "deeply planted." I like this because there is a difference between things that have been shallowly planted and deeply planted. I could plant a small tree in front of my house and not dig a very deep hole for it. Then, when a storm came, the tree might be uprooted because its roots were too shallow. In contrast, if I had a fully grown oak tree that had been in my yard for decades and its root system reached deep into the ground, I would be more confident that tree would be able to withstand storms or strong winds. The way to stand firm in faith is to be deeply planted and to grow deep roots in

Christ. Anything that is deeply rooted also gets built up and strengthened, as Colossians 2:7 indicates. When the summer has been very hot with little rain, a deeply rooted tree can still find water deep in the earth, where its roots are. Younger trees without deep roots may not survive a hot, dry summer.

No one has ever heard enough of God's Word. Everyone needs more and more of it, every day. It always strengthens us, always helps us, and always leads us to victory.

The Old Testament prophet Jeremiah uses this analogy when he contrasts a person who is not deeply rooted in Christ, but who trusts in the flesh instead, with a person who is deeply rooted in their trust in the Lord:

> This is what the LORD says: "Cursed is the one who trusts in man, who draws strength from mere flesh and whose heart turns away from the LORD. That person will be like a bush in the wastelands; they will not see prosperity when it comes. They will dwell in the parched places of the desert, in a salt land where no one lives.
>
> But blessed is the one who trusts in the LORD, whose confidence is in him. *They will be like a tree planted by the water* that sends out its roots by the stream. It does not fear when heat comes; its leaves are always green. It has no worries in a year of drought and never fails to bear fruit.
>
> Jeremiah 17:5–8 (emphasis mine)

The Amplified Bible, Classic Edition of Jeremiah 17:7 says, "[*Most*] *blessed*" is the person "who believes in, trusts in, *and* relies on the Lord" (emphasis mine), and the Amplified Bible says that person is "blessed [with spiritual security]." This verse is not talking about simply being blessed, but "most blessed with spiritual security," and being secure at all times is a wonderful blessing.

A third reason I like the Amplified Bible, Classic Edition rendering of Colossians 2:7 is that when it says we are to be "continually built up" in Christ, it goes on to say, "becoming increasingly more confirmed *and* established in the faith." We become more and more established in our faith by constantly reminding ourselves of what God's Word says, by studying it repeatedly, and by hearing it and speaking it over and over again. Hebrews 4:12 says: "For the word of God is alive and active. Sharper than any double-edged sword, it penetrates even to dividing soul and spirit, joints and marrow; it judges the thoughts and attitudes of the heart." The fact that God's Word is "alive and active" tells us that there is always something new to discover in it. It is a living Word, full of power. We may read a verse or passage for years—even memorize it—and suddenly one day we read it again and learn something new and different from it.

People may have lived twenty years with hatred in their heart and never realized it was hurting them and their relationship with God. But when they see in the Word of God that we are to forgive our enemies even as Christ forgives us, suddenly they have discovered a treasure that will be life-changing if they obey the Word they have received.

I encourage you to study God's Word with enthusiasm, as if

you are expecting to find some information that is really going to help you. Take each thing you study personally and as if the Holy Spirit inspired the writing of the Bible just for you.

Personal Reflection

What can you do to grow in your faith and become more deeply rooted in Christ?

_____

_____

_____

_____

_____

_____

Overflowing with Thankfulness

Paul also encourages his readers to overflow with thankfulness. We know from this and other epistles that he understands the power of being thankful. He writes in 1 Thessalonians 5:18: "Give thanks in all circumstances; for this is God's will for you in Christ Jesus." This means that no matter what is happening, we are to be thankful. "All circumstances" means *all circumstances*, not just the ones that are easy or the ones that make us happy. And in Philippians 4:6, we see that when we ask God for something, we are to do so "with thanksgiving." There was a time when I was studying this verse that I felt God say to me, "If you are complaining about what you already have, why should I give you more to complain about?" We are not to complain about anything, but to be thankful in every situation. God answers prayers prayed in faith, not complaints made with a bad attitude.

You will see as you continue through this study that Paul mentions thanksgiving several times in Colossians (1:3, 3:15, 3:17, 4:2) in addition to these words in Colossians 2, so we know that he thought being thankful was very important. Being thankful is a positive attitude that produces positive results. It is the opposite of complaining, which comes from a negative mindset and produces undesired results. Constant complaining and focusing on what is wrong in a situation instead of what is right keeps us trapped in our problems. But praise and thanksgiving lift us out of our struggles. An easy way to obey the Word of God each day is to let your heart overflow with thanksgiving in every circumstance. Form a habit of being thankful and saying so (Ps. 100:4). Voice your gratitude to God and others who help or bless you.

Personal Reflection

How can you be more consistent in being thankful at all times, in every situation?

_____

_____

_____

_____

_____

_____

_____

CHAPTER 9

DON'T BE TAKEN CAPTIVE

The Only True Foundation of Truth

Colossians 2:8–10

See to it that no one takes you captive through hollow
and deceptive philosophy, which depends on human
tradition and the elemental spiritual forces of this world
rather than on Christ. For in Christ all the fullness of
the Deity lives in bodily form, and in Christ you have
been brought to fullness. He is the head over every
power and authority.

Society today is full of philosophy, and when we hear that
someone is a philosopher, it can sound quite impressive. But
when I looked up the definition of *philosopher*, I discovered
that a philosopher is simply a thinker. Therefore, we can
define philosophy as simply a way of thinking about or view-
ing things.

The Internet has made spreading thoughts, ideas, and
information faster and easier than ever. People can publi-
cize their philosophies and gain a following very quickly if
their ideas are appealing. There are political philosophies,
economic philosophies, religious philosophies, philosophies
of relationships (such as how the two genders should relate
to each other, what constitutes a family, and how marriages

and families should operate), and many other types of philosophies.

People can have the philosophy that lying, cheating, and stealing are acceptable. They can think they should live only for the present and not worry about taking care of their physical bodies or preparing wisely for the future. They can have the philosophy that they should not have to work or earn anything for themselves—that everything should be given to them. Almost anyone can find a philosophy that agrees with the way they think—or they can invent one.

Paul writes that such philosophies—ones not based on the truth of Christ—are dangerous and can even take people captive. To be captive means to lose freedom and become subject to someone else's authority. Jesus wants to be the only authority in our lives, and when we allow Him to be in that rightful place, He gives us freedom.

Any philosophy that goes against God's truth has its roots in the enemy. The enemy is a liar (John 8:44), he is the deceiver (Rev. 12:9), and he constantly tries to get us to believe things that are not true. Sometimes what he gets us to believe is not categorically untrue; there is just enough nonsense mixed in with it that it makes it not true. The only way we can ever avoid being deceived is to pray regularly that we shall not be deceived and to stay in God's Word, which is full of truth.

Personal Reflection

What philosophies or belief systems are prevalent around you right now, and how can you strengthen yourself against them with the Word of God?

_____

_____

_____

_____

_____

_____

_____

A prevalent philosophy today says that there is no firm, exact, or absolute truth and that everything is relative. I cringe inside when I hear that. People who talk about it say that the generation living today is different than previous generations. They declare that we are now living in the twenty-first century and that, in fact, everything is different. Yes, I agree that some things are different, but God's Word has not changed. No matter what century people live in, the Word of God is still the only truth that sets us free (John 8:32), and it is the only thing that will work in our lives. Isaiah prophesied thousands of years ago: "The grass withers and the flowers fall, but the word of our God endures forever" (Isa. 40:8).

Paul knows that only God's truth can stand against the world's thought systems. He issues a clear warning to his readers, urging them not to let philosophies or ways of thinking take them captive. He refers to these as "hollow and deceptive philosophy" and says that they depend on human beings and the natural world instead of having their basis in Christ. Only in Christ, Paul declares, does the fullness of God dwell, and only in Him will human beings ever be full and complete.

Trying to find satisfaction in any school of thought or belief system not rooted in the Word of God will always leave people empty and frustrated, and trying to add other philosophies to the Word of God will only lead to confusion. We need to be single-minded in our commitment to God's Word and to base all of our thoughts and belief systems on its truth. Jesus reigns over every philosophy and every way of thinking anyone could imagine. God has given Him all authority in heaven and on earth (Matt. 28:18), and He satisfies completely.

Personal Reflection

How have you been tempted to embrace the philosophies the world offers?

_____

_____

_____

_____

_____

_____

_____

Christ's Victory

Colossians 2:11–15

In him you were also circumcised with a circumcision not performed by human hands. Your whole self ruled by the flesh was put off when you were circumcised by Christ, having been buried with him in baptism, in which you were also raised with him through your faith in the working of God, who raised him from the dead. When you were dead in your sins and in the uncircumcision of your flesh, God made you alive with Christ. He forgave us all our sins, having canceled the charge of our legal indebtedness, which stood against us and condemned us; he has taken it away, nailing it to the cross. And having disarmed the powers and authorities, he made a public spectacle of them, triumphing over them by the cross.

The first thing we notice in Colossians 2:11–15 is that the self is "ruled by the flesh." The flesh always wants its own way, which is contrary to God's way. Paul explains in Galatians 5 the battle between a person's flesh and the Spirit of God who lives in us:

So I say, walk by the Spirit, and you will not gratify the desires of the flesh. For the flesh desires what is contrary to the Spirit, and the Spirit what is contrary to the flesh. They are in conflict with each other, so that you are not to do whatever you want. But if you are led by the Spirit, you are not under the law...Those who belong to Christ Jesus have crucified the flesh with its passions and desires. Since we live by the Spirit, let us keep in step with the Spirit.

Galatians 5:16–18, 24–25

Following the flesh leads to death, but following the Spirit leads to life. This passage causes us to wonder what actually happened when Jesus died and was raised again. According to Romans 6:6, spiritually speaking, when He died for our sins, we died with Him. We died to sin. Sin itself did not die; we died to it. This is why inside every born-again believer there is something that wants to please God, something that does not want to do wrong.

When we are born again, our hearts are circumcised. This is not circumcision in the flesh, which was required of the males in Old Testament Israel; this is a spiritual circumcision of the heart (Rom. 2:25–29). If the heart is right, the person will want to make right choices because doing what is right makes us alive in Christ. We died with Christ, meaning that we are dead to sin and the old nature, but we have also been resurrected with Him, according to Colossians 2:12.

This does not mean that we never have a desire to sin. It means the desire to sin is a fleshly desire, which can be resisted and overcome by living in the reality of our new nature and the resurrection life. Just think how amazing it is: Because of what Jesus has done for us, all of our sins are forgiven and the penalty for them is paid. Jesus paid the debt we owed for our many sins and misdeeds, and He removed the condemnation. Now, we simply need to walk in this amazing truth.

At the cross, Jesus totally disarmed the ruling powers and authorities, meaning He took their power and authority away from them. Satan—and all his demons—are completely powerless over those who are in Christ. If you are a believer, they have no authority in your life unless you give it to them through unbelief or disobedience. In Christ, you have victory over them. You can receive any ground you have lost due to lack of knowledge or sin. All you need to do is sincerely repent of your sin and begin immediately to do the right thing.

For example, Paul wrote in his letter to the Ephesians that if they let the sun set on their anger, they would give the devil a foothold in their lives (Eph. 4:26–27). Anyone who realizes they are guilty of this can repent and forgive those with whom they are angry—and then Satan loses the ground he has taken. The good news is that in Christ we can always have a new beginning. It is never too late to begin again.

The Reality in Christ

Colossians 2:16–17

Therefore do not let anyone judge you by what you eat or drink, or with regard to a religious festival, a New Moon celebration or a Sabbath day. These are a shadow of the things that were to come; the reality, however, is found in Christ.

This passage follows Colossians 2:15, which affirms the fact that Jesus triumphed over all powers and authorities and rendered them impotent in the lives of believers. Paul is saying here that because we are raised to new life with Christ and because nothing has power over us and we belong to God, no one can judge us. These Old Testament things were shadows; they pointed us toward New Testament realities that would be fulfilled in Christ. He fulfilled every point of the Old Testament law and set us free from its rules and regulations.

When we say we have been set free from the law, *it does not mean we are free from the moral and ethical laws of God's Word.* It means we no longer live under the Law of Moses—the Old Testament rules and regulations. Parts of the Mosaic Law specified how people could approach God. They had to wash themselves in certain ways and go through various rituals before they could even talk to God. Even then, they were not allowed to speak with Him personally. They had to talk to Him through a priest. But when Jesus died and the veil in the temple split from top to bottom (Mark 15:38), it signified that God was opening the new and living way we read about in Hebrews 10:10–22. It said to everyone, "Because of Christ, you can now come to God yourself. You don't have to rely on anyone else to speak to Him for you. You can have your own personal relationship with Him."

Here Paul encourages believers to find freedom in Christ rather than try to relate to God and please Him by obeying religious rules and regulations. Paul's epistle to the Galatians includes much wisdom about freedom from this kind of legalism, and if you want to learn more, you can find it in my Biblical Study series book on Galatians.

The Critical Judgment of the Proud

Colossians 2:18–19

Do not let anyone who delights in false humility and the worship of angels disqualify you. Such a person also goes into great detail about what they have seen; they are puffed up with idle notions by their unspiritual mind. They have lost connection with the head, from whom the whole body, supported and held together by its ligaments and sinews, grows as God causes it to grow.

Some people are proud of themselves because they follow all the rules and regulations that they believe qualify them for acceptance by God. These people often disqualify anyone who doesn't do what they do. In their pride, they assume they should be giving instructions to everyone else and are quick to criticize those who do not follow them. People like this are often mean-spirited and never show mercy to anyone. They are not taking their direction from Christ, who is the head of the church, for they have no true connection with Him. Jesus calls these people "whitewashed tombs, which look beautiful on the outside but on the inside are full of the bones of the dead and everything unclean" (Matt. 23:27).

He calls them hypocrites and blind guides, and refers to them as those who follow the letter of the law but won't lift a finger to help anyone in need. His attitude toward those who are rule keepers but have unclean hearts is clear and should encourage us to make sure that anything we do is done for right reasons—out of our love for God and not to impress people or feel superior to them.

Love for God Inspires Self-Control

Colossians 2:20–23

Since you died with Christ to the elemental spiritual forces of this world, why, as though you still belonged to the world, do you submit to its rules: "Do not handle! Do not taste! Do not touch!"? These rules, which have to do with things that are all destined to perish with use, are based on merely human commands and teachings. Such regulations indeed have an appearance of wisdom, with their self-imposed worship, their false humility and their harsh treatment of the body, but they lack any value in restraining sensual indulgence.

Paul makes reference here to the rules and regulations of the world. Trying to follow rules and regulations will always frustrate us. Instead of striving to obey them, we would be wise to obey Christ and embrace the freedom He offers us, allowing Him to strengthen us to live the way God would have us live.

Always keep in mind that no degree of following man-made rules has the ability to restrain our fleshly desires. Only love for God and appreciation for all He has done for us in Christ will provoke us to use self-control and empower us to choose to walk in the Spirit rather than the flesh.

CHAPTER 10

---◦---

HOW TO THINK AND ACT AS A CHRISTIAN

Set Your Mind in the Right Direction

Colossians 3:1–4

*Since, then, you have been raised with Christ, set your
hearts on things above, where Christ is, seated at the
right hand of God. Set your minds on things above, not
on earthly things. For you died, and your life is now
hidden with Christ in God. When Christ, who is your life,
appears, then you also will appear with him in glory.*

Everyone who has been born again has also been raised with
Christ, and Paul has a specific instruction for us in Colossians
3:1–2. I have taught this passage for years from the Amplified
Bible, Classic Edition, so I want you to see what that says:

If then you have been raised with Christ [to a new life,
thus sharing His resurrection from the dead], aim at *and*
seek the [rich, eternal treasures] that are above, where
Christ is, seated at the right hand of God. And set your
minds *and* keep them set on what is above (the higher
things), not on the things that are on the earth.

Those of us who have been raised with Christ are to "aim
at and seek" things that are above, or as the NIV says, "set our
hearts on" them. I like the use of the word *seek* in this verse

because if we study the original term in the Greek language, we see that it means "to crave, to pursue, and to go after with all your might." In order to stay strong in faith day after day, week after week, year after year, we really *must* seek God.

Some people today feel they have done what they should do spiritually if they go to church on Sundays. But in the days in which we live, that is not enough to keep us strong all week long. Plus, we cannot expect someone else—a loving mother or father, a good friend, a spouse, or even a pastor—to seek God for us. The only way to be strong in God is to spend time with Him.

Don't be satisfied with a secondhand relationship with God. That means don't depend on someone else's faith to keep you in the right place with God. Instead, have your own personal, intimate relationship with Him.

Personal Reflection

What kind of spiritual habits have you formed that help you stay close to God?

_____

_____

_____

_____

_____

Set Your Mind and Keep It Set

Paul continues his instructions with a verse I have taught on often because I believe it is so important. He says to "set your minds on things above." The Amplified Bible, Classic Edition reads, "And set your minds *and keep them set* on what is above" (emphasis mine). Setting our minds on the right thing once or twice won't do us much good, but if we set them in the right direction and keep them set, we will be victorious.

When Paul urges us to set our minds and keep them set "on things above," he is not simply telling us to prepare for the day we will go to heaven or to envision the pearly gates. He means that if we want to live a high life—a life that honors God—we cannot think about things that are low, base, common, or ungodly. We need to put our minds where we want our lives to be, because our lives will follow where our thoughts lead. According to Proverbs 23:7, however we think in our hearts, that's how we will turn out. I always say, "Where the mind goes, the man follows."

To help us understand what it means on a practical level for us to think about "things above," meaning right and excellent things, let me start by listing some low things people often think about. Thinking about what you don't have, instead of what you do have, is a low thing. Thinking about people who have things you would like and saying they don't deserve them is low. Thoughts of jealousy, pride, anger, comparison, and judgment are low, as is holding grudges against people instead of forgiving them. Focusing on your faults instead of your strengths is low, and so is wallowing in self-pity and feeling condemned about your past mistakes.

Of course, high thinking is the opposite of low thinking. When your thoughts are set on things above, you thank God for every blessing you do have instead of complaining about what you don't have. You rejoice with others over their successes instead of being envious. You encourage people who are pursuing what you would like to do or what you would like to have instead of secretly hoping they don't get it. You choose peace over anger, humility over pride, mercy over judgment, and forgiveness over unforgiveness. You pray instead of worrying; you trust God in every situation instead of taking matters into your own hands; you stand firm in faith that God has a bright future for you instead of feeling guilty over your past. There are many other ways to think high thoughts, and I believe these examples will help you know how to do that.

I hope you will always remember how powerful your thoughts are. A made-up mind is very powerful. What you think about will determine the quality of your life. When you think happy thoughts, you live a happy life. Don't let the devil control your thinking; do your own thinking. Think according to God's Word and believe the best of everyone.

Once you have set your mind on something, it's important to keep it set and to not doubt yourself or become double-minded. This is how you defeat the devil on the battlefield of the mind. The apostle James says, "The one who doubts is like a wave of the sea, blown and tossed by the wind...

Such a person is double-minded and unstable in all they do"
(James 1:6, 8). Once you have explored your options, prayed,
sought God's will, and made a decision in a matter, you can
set your mind firmly on that course of action. You have to
reach the point where you know what you plan to do is the
right thing and say, "My mind is made up. With God's help,
this is what I'm going to do, and it will produce good results
in my life." When you have a made-up mind and you are a
born-again person with the Holy Spirit to help you, there is
nothing you cannot do through Christ. You probably won't
have victory overnight, but you will have it eventually if you
don't give up.

Personal Reflection

In what specific areas of your life do you need to set
your mind and keep it set?

_____

_____

_____

_____

_____

_____

Put Old Ways behind You

Colossians 3:5–11

Put to death, therefore, whatever belongs to your earthly nature: sexual immorality, impurity, lust, evil desires and greed, which is idolatry. Because of these, the wrath of God is coming. You used to walk in these ways, in the life you once lived. But now you must also rid yourselves of all such things as these: anger, rage, malice, slander, and filthy language from your lips. Do not lie to each other, since you have taken off your old self with its practices and have put on the new self, which is being renewed in knowledge in the image of its Creator. Here there is no Gentile or Jew, circumcised or uncircumcised, barbarian, Scythian, slave or free, but Christ is all, and is in all.

This passage lists specific behaviors and speech that people who love Jesus cannot allow in their lives. To put this in spiritual terms, it talks about crucifying the flesh and dying to self. All believers are called to do this. Paul writes that he personally knows what this means: "May I never boast except in the cross of our Lord Jesus Christ, through which the world has been crucified to me, and I to the world" (Gal. 6:14). And in Galatians 2:20 he says, "I have been crucified with Christ and I no longer live, but Christ lives in me." Spiritually speaking, this has already been accomplished. It happened when Christ died and rose from the dead, and now we are in the process of learning how to walk in what He purchased for us with His blood.

When people read these verses, especially if they have not been Christians for very long, they think, *Imagine putting to death all those negative things! That must be so wonderful!* And then they think, *I'm just not there yet. I don't even think I'm close!* They don't always realize that Paul had been a Christian for twenty years by the time he wrote these words. That should give everyone hope. The question is not whether or not we have "arrived" and can say what Paul says. It is: Are we growing? We don't please God by doing everything perfectly all the time. We please God by having faith and wanting to mature in Him. Always remember that a person with a right heart who makes some mistakes is more important to God than a person with perfect behavior and an impure heart.

Paul uses strong language in Colossians 3:5–11 when he says, "Put to death." He is not encouraging violence against yourself, but he is trying to make the point that sin must be dealt with strongly. When we know we have sin in our lives, the first important thing to do is repent of it and begin praying regularly that God will strengthen you and enable you to say no when that temptation comes. If a specific person is tempting you to sin, you may have to remove them from your life. If you have a job that requires you to do things that you know are wrong, you should get another job. If you are overweight or unhealthy and candy is a big temptation to you, then don't buy it and take it home. When God shows you an action to take, it is important to obey Him. Obedience to God is the adjustment of anything in our lives that is out of harmony with Him.

The best way I know to crucify the flesh in your practical, everyday life is simply not to feed it. You can kill anything if you starve it. Every time we give in to a fleshly whim or desire, we feed the flesh. But each time we resist fleshly temptations, the fleshly trait becomes weaker and weaker until it eventually dies.

Personal Reflection

How can you feed the things of the Spirit and starve the things of the flesh in practical ways in your life?

_____

_____

_____

_____

_____

_____

Paul concludes this passage with a reminder to his readers that the reason for putting on the new self today is that, in Christ, they have put off the old self. This reminds us of 2 Corinthians 5:17. I have already commented on that verse, but let me say here that this idea of putting off the old, putting on the new, and being a new creation in Christ can be confusing.

People wonder, "If I have been given all of these good things and this new life, why am I not seeing it? Why do I struggle to act better?" The answer is simple. What has been legally given to us through the blood of Christ and what we experience in our lives can be very different unless we have learned to walk out what God has done in our lives.

Here is an example that people usually relate to. We bought our son a car when he was fourteen because we found a good deal on a perfect car for him. Though it was his car, he couldn't drive it because he didn't know how to drive and wasn't old enough to get a license.

We are often that way with the things Jesus has already provided for us. They are ours and that is the truth, but the fact is that we are still learning and growing.

I encourage you to be patient when you want to change and do not see it happening as quickly as you would like. If you keep praying, keep walking with God, keep learning who you are in Christ, keep obeying and meditating on His Word, change will come. We belong to Christ, and we are called to live set-apart lives. This simply means that we will not be able to live a life that pleases God and also do everything the world does. God has called us to a higher life, and any sacrifice we think we are making to have that life is well worth the benefits.

CHAPTER 11

◆—◦—◆

SPIRITUAL CLOTHING

Dressing Yourself to Reflect the Image of Christ

Colossians 3:12–13

Therefore, as God's chosen people, holy and dearly loved, clothe yourselves with compassion, kindness, humility, gentleness and patience. Bear with each other and forgive one another if any of you has a grievance against someone. Forgive as the Lord forgave you.

I like to say that Colossians 3:12–14 is about our "spiritual clothing." In Colossians 3:10 Paul mentions putting on "the new self," and Colossians 3:12 describes people who manifest the new self. Before I comment on each piece of our spiritual clothing individually, let me say that generally speaking, putting on our spiritual clothing simply means that we approach each day with the attitude that says, "God, I don't want any trouble today. I hope everything goes my way, but experience has taught me that it doesn't always happen. If it doesn't, help me to endure whatever comes my way with good temper. And help me to be kind, gentle, and patient toward everyone I meet." These verses encourage us to be like Jesus in our behavior.

Looking at Colossians 3:12 closely, first we see that Paul says we are "chosen people, holy and dearly loved." You may remember from my commentary on Colossians 1:2, when

Paul addresses this letter "to God's holy people in Colossae," that to be called *holy* or *chosen* is similar to being called "consecrated," which means to be set apart for God's purposes. So Paul appeals here to God's set-apart people and reminds us that we are dearly loved. Anytime we are tempted to doubt God's love, we need look no further than the cross, where He sent His only Son to be punished, to die in our place, and to forgive our sins, making it possible for us to live in close, personal, right relationship with Him.

The spiritual clothing we can wear includes "compassion, kindness, humility, gentleness and patience." Kindness, gentleness, and patience are mentioned as fruit of the Holy Spirit (Gal. 5:22–23). Jesus demonstrated these qualities, along with humility and compassion, during His ministry. Often in the Gospels, we read that He had compassion for individuals and groups of people and extended kindness to them (Matt. 9:36, 14:14, 20:34; Luke 7:13). Philippians 2:5–8 characterizes His humility, and Paul appealed to the Corinthians "by the humility and gentleness of Christ" (2 Cor. 10:1). We also read about His patience when Paul writes, "But for that very reason I was shown mercy so that in me, the worst of sinners, Christ Jesus might display his immense patience as an example for those who would believe in him and receive eternal life" (1 Tim. 1:16).

Personal Reflection

Which specific aspects of your spiritual clothing do you most need to put on and demonstrate in your everyday life?

_____

_____

_____

_____

_____

_____

Bear with and Forgive Others

People who wear the right spiritual clothing also bear with and forgive others. Many times each day, we can find reasons to be offended. We may have ample opportunity to be frustrated or even angry with coworkers, neighbors, friends, and family members, or we can become aggravated by total strangers who do things such as cut us off in traffic or bump into us in the checkout line at the grocery store. We can even be upset by the news. But spiritually mature people have the ability, through Christ, to be forbearing and to extend grace to others. One of the best responses we can have toward people and things that normally upset us is to hold on to our peace and pray about the situations we have encountered. It is especially powerful to be willing to pray for the person who has hurt or offended us.

One way I have heard forgiveness explained is to "let it go" or "drop it." Do you have anything you are carrying that you need to let go of or drop?

Most of us can behave in godly ways as long as we are having quiet time alone, maybe drinking coffee, reading our Bibles, and praying at home. It's easy when we're by ourselves. But as soon as we start having to deal with other people, it gets more difficult. If you are like many people, you won't be very far along in your day before someone does something you do not like. That's when you have a chance to demonstrate spiritual maturity or spiritual immaturity. Anyone can be nice and pleasant to people who do not cause them trouble. But it takes God's power—the love of God inside of you—to be forgiving, kind, and gentle when you are frustrated with someone or something.

This is a practical example of setting your mind and keeping it set. You can set your mind each day by saying, "I have decided that I can handle anything that comes up today through Christ, who is my strength, and that with His help I will treat people well." If you determine in advance to keep that mindset throughout the day, then every time something isn't perfect, it will not upset you. You will simply recognize those challenges as opportunities to rely on the strength of Christ that is in you. At the end of the day, you will look back on it and realize that you stayed calm, steady, patient, and kind. That will be a powerful witness to the people around you.

Perhaps the best-known passage about what we are to "put on" as believers is in Ephesians 6:13–17:

> Therefore put on the full armor of God, so that when the day of evil comes, you may be able to stand your ground, and after you have done everything, to stand. Stand firm then, with the belt of truth buckled around your waist, with the breastplate of righteousness in place, and with your feet fitted with the readiness that comes from the gospel of peace. In addition to all this, take up the shield of faith, with which you can extinguish all the flaming arrows of the evil one. Take the helmet of salvation and the sword of the Spirit, which is the word of God.

These things, like the ones in Colossians 3:12–14, are not tangible items we can pull out of our closets. They are spiritual. They are mindsets, attitudes, and behaviors that determine how we will live. This right kind of behavior doesn't just magically appear through us. We have to choose to put it on.

Many people, especially women, spend a lot of time getting ready for each day. We choose our clothes and accessories carefully, we work on our hair until it's just right, and we apply our makeup meticulously. A lot of us would never consider leaving the house without feeling properly dressed for the day.

But many people don't even think about getting dressed spiritually. I don't know about you, but I may change clothes two or three times in order to be sure that what I am wearing looks good on me. We should consider that some behaviors simply don't look good on God's children, and just as we change our clothing if it doesn't look right or fit well, we should be prepared to change our behavior if it doesn't fit us or look becoming on us.

We can tell from Colossians 3:12–14 and from Ephesians 6:13–17 that Paul viewed spiritual preparation as important. The point of all of this is to say that no matter how good we may look on the outside, our inner life is what really matters. If people go through each day angry or jealous or prideful on the inside, those qualities will be evident to those they meet. But when a person's inner life is characterized by kindness, gentleness, humility, righteousness, peace, and other godly attributes, those will also be evident. Things will not go well for us on the outside if we are not right on the inside.

Personal Reflection

Describe an experience—positive or negative—when what was inside of you strongly affected what came out of you in your words or actions.

_____

_____

_____

_____

_____

_____

I want to mention one more verse before we close this section. In Revelation 16:15, Jesus says: "Look, I come like a thief! Blessed is the one who stays awake and remains clothed, so as not to go naked and be shamefully exposed." If we do not understand the idea of spiritual clothing, this verse may be confusing to us. In it, Jesus is talking about remaining spiritually clothed so you are spiritually protected, not vulnerable to the enemy. I have said when teaching on this verse that the devil doesn't care what color your outfit is, but he hates to see you dressed in the knowledge of who you are in Christ, representing Jesus in all you do. To stay strong in faith, resist the enemy, and be an effective witness for Christ, it is vital to remain spiritually clothed all the time.

Put on Love

Colossians 3:14

And over all these virtues put on love, which binds them all together in perfect unity.

Paul writes that over all other virtues, we are to put on love. Our primary goal in life should not be to get everything we want, but to walk in love. Loving God and other people is at the top of the Bible's list of things that are important. We should also love ourselves in a manner that is pleasing to God, and that simply means that we receive the love God has for us. If love is the most important thing for us to put on, then it is something we should pay close attention to. Love is not merely an emotional feeling, but it is a choice we make about how we will treat people. When I say "people" I mean all people, not just the ones who are easy for us to be with.

Every once in a while, I lose something in my closet when I want to wear it. I know it is in my closet, but I can't find it. I think love may be like that for some of us. We know we have it in us, but somehow we can't find it. If what I have lost or misplaced is important enough to me, I don't stop looking until I find it. If love is important to us, we will seek it until we find it and we will put it on.

CHAPTER 12

BE AT PEACE

Follow the Umpire of Your Soul

Colossians 3:15

Let the peace of Christ rule in your hearts, since as members
of one body you were called to peace. And be thankful.

Colossians 3:15 is another verse I studied and taught on for
years from the Amplified Bible, Classic Edition:

And let the peace (soul harmony which comes) from Christ
rule (act as umpire continually) in your hearts [deciding
and settling with finality all questions that arise in your
minds, in that peaceful state] to which as [members of
Christ's] one body you were also called [to live]. And be
thankful (appreciative), [giving praise to God always].

I like this version of this verse because the idea of peace
as an umpire in our hearts helps us understand so well how
God uses His gift of peace in our lives. In a game of base-
ball, the umpire is the one who has the final say concerning
whether a player is "safe" or "out." If the player is safe, he can
stay in the game and keep playing. If he is out, he cannot play
anymore, at least for a while. Peace is like an umpire; it lets
us know what should be kept in our lives and what should be
out. The Bible tells us that "God is not a God of disorder but

of peace" (1 Cor. 14:33) and that Jesus "himself is our peace" (Eph. 2:14). When God gives us peace about something in our lives, we know it is the right thing for us to do, and when He doesn't give us peace, we know it is wrong for us.

We desperately need to learn to follow peace when we make decisions. Many people make decisions based on what they *want* to do or what they *think* seems good. But neither one of those is a reliable source of information. Human desire can be very strong, so it is extremely important that we submit our desires to the leading of the Holy Spirit. Only He knows what is best for us.

It is possible to get so excited about something that you can talk yourself into doing it and push to make it happen, even if it really is not a great idea. Psalm 127:1 says, "Unless the LORD builds the house, the builders labor in vain." It doesn't say the builders cannot build it, but that their hard work is fruitless.

When we feel very excited about something, our enthusiasm can override any lack of peace we may sense deep in our hearts. I have learned that when I am unusually excited about something, the best course of action for me is not to act right away. It's smarter for me to wait a little while and let the enthusiasm settle down and then see what I think about the situation. Sometimes I feel peace and move ahead; sometimes I don't. But at least I give myself a chance to see if peace is there or not.

If you have ever paid the price for moving forward with a decision when you did not have peace about it, you know what I mean. It could be something as simple as buying something you really, really wanted, even though something inside you said not to do it. Or it could be something as complicated as getting deeply involved in a relationship that affected several people when you knew in your heart it was not right. When we fail to follow peace and then have to live with the consequences of that decision, it helps us learn to be led by peace in the future.

Personal Reflection

When have you sensed a lack of peace about something but moved forward with it anyway? What did you learn from that?

_____

_____

_____

_____

_____

Peace is one of the primary ways we hear from God. People often ask, "How can I hear from God? How can I know what God's will is?" God leads us many different ways, and when He leads us, we have a deep sense of peace in our hearts about the direction in which He wants us to go. Our flesh may not like everything about it, but the peace in our hearts, or the lack of it, will tell us what is right.

Let the Word Dwell in You

Colossians 3:16

Let the message of Christ dwell among you richly as you
teach and admonish one another with all wisdom through
psalms, hymns, and songs from the Spirit, singing to God
with gratitude in your hearts.

This verse is not talking about singing to each other as much as it is talking about keeping your heart happy, your thoughts disciplined, and your life simple. All of these add to our peace. I'm not very good at singing, but I find myself humming often throughout the day, which Ephesians 5:19 calls "making melody in your heart to the Lord" (NKJV). Making melody in your heart to Him keeps negative emotions and attitudes out of your heart, and that's always good.

Colossians 3:16 in the New International Version says to "let the message of Christ dwell among you richly," but many other translations render it as "let the word of Christ dwell in you richly." In other words, let the Word of God fill your thoughts. Think about and meditate on what God says.

Let me encourage you to ask yourself how much time you spend each day letting Scripture roll over and over in your mind. You may often hear, "Meditate on the Word," but hearing that will not help you if you do not actually do it. One of the best ways to become rooted and grounded in the truth of a Bible verse or passage is to take just one or two of them and, throughout the day, meditate on and think about what they mean. As I mentioned in my commentary on Colossians 1:27, the only way to experience the full benefit of all that God's Word offers is to meditate on it, just as the only way to get the full benefit of the food you eat is to chew it well.

Personal Reflection

Which specific Scripture verse or passage will you begin to meditate on right now?

_____

_____

_____

_____

_____

_____

The verse also talks about admonishing one another. Most people do not like to be admonished or be told what they are doing wrong. But here Paul teaches us that when correction is necessary, it is to be done with wisdom and by a person in whom God's Word dwells. No one wants to be corrected when they're gossiping, when they aren't acting honestly, when they are spreading rumors, or when their anger is out of control. But in certain situations, and in the right spirit, admonishment helps people grow and mature spiritually.

CHAPTER 13

—◦◦◦—

DO EVERYTHING IN JESUS' NAME AND FOR HIM

Determining What's Pleasing to God

Colossians 3:17

And whatever you do, whether in word or deed, do it all in the name of the Lord Jesus, giving thanks to God the Father through him.

Some people give no thought to God when they decide how to spend their time, how to spend their money, how to dress, how to think, how to speak, or who they are in relationship with. They simply do what they want to do.

But Colossians 3:17 says to do *everything* in Jesus' name. Let me ask you: If you were to think about all the plans you have for today, would each one be pleasing to God? Can you say that you will go to work today and do your very best, handling every situation with integrity and treating everyone around you well because you are working in Jesus' name? Would you be okay with Jesus overhearing your conversation in the break room or with your spouse when you get home? Is the movie you are planning to watch tonight something you would want Jesus to see you watching?

Notice also in this verse that Paul says we are to give thanks while we do things in Jesus' name. Are you thankful when you enjoy what you are doing even when it is difficult? When I wrote earlier in this book that Colossians has much to say about the practical aspects of our lives as Christians, this is what I am talking about. God cares about every single thing we are involved in. He wants us to depend on Him to lead us and to honor and glorify Him in all we do.

This verse also encourages us to give thanks to God. I believe that praise and thanksgiving protect us from the enemy and his plan. We read about this in Deuteronomy 28:47–48. Simply being thankful sends the enemy away. No matter how you feel—afraid, discouraged, hurt, exhausted— let me encourage you to pause right now and spend a minute thanking God for all the good things He has done, is doing, and will do in your life. We can never be reminded too often to voice our thankfulness. It seems that complaining comes naturally, but we must choose to put on a thankful attitude. The more often we are reminded of something, the more likely we are to do it.

Christian Relationships

Colossians 3:18–22

Wives, submit yourselves to your husbands, as is fitting in the Lord. Husbands, love your wives and do not be harsh with them. Children, obey your parents in everything, for this pleases the Lord. Fathers, do not embitter your children, or they will become discouraged. Slaves, obey your earthly masters in everything; and do it, not only when their eye is on you and to curry their favor, but with sincerity of heart and reverence for the Lord.

Some people get nervous when they read this passage because it starts with "Wives, submit yourselves to your husbands." Some teaching focuses on that idea excessively, but when I teach on it, I like to include it as part of the five verses of Colossians 3:18–22. The heart of the passage is that people need to treat each other well. Followers of Christ need to incorporate each part of this passage that relates to them into their daily lives.

Wives do need to submit to their husbands, "as is fitting in the Lord," and husbands do need to love their wives and be kind to them. Children do need to be obedient, and parents don't need to do things that will anger or embitter their children. Every time I teach on this passage, someone asks the same question: What does a woman do when her husband does not treat her as the Bible instructs? My answer is this: Two wrongs never make anything right. Each of us is responsible to do the right thing regardless of what others are doing.

I cannot fully answer the question about what wives should do if their husbands are not treating them right in this book because each person's situation is different. In some cases, women simply are not happy in their marriages or they are struggling with their husband's personality, while in other situations, serious abuse may be taking place. I would encourage anyone who is being abused to seek help from a pastor or counselor. God has not called anyone to suffer abuse in the name of submission, but the answer may be as simple as confronting the person who is abusive. Once again, let me urge you not to isolate yourself and merely put up with being abused. Talk to someone and get the advice and help you need.

Colossians 3:18–21 pertains to marriage and family relationships, and verse 22 focuses on work relationships and doing everything we do with reverence for the Lord. No matter where you work or whether you like your job, it's important for you as a Christian to go to work each day with the idea that you are there to serve God. God has given you that job, and you are to do it to the best of your ability, applying all the principles you believe would please God, such as being excellent, having honesty and integrity, respecting your boss, and treating others well. You don't look for ways to take shortcuts; you don't work when your employer is looking and make personal phone calls and play games on the Internet when he isn't; you don't take office supplies home to use on your child's school project. I could go on, but I believe you know what I mean.

Remember that this passage is located close to Colossians 3:15, which encourages us to live in peace. Because of that, I believe the point of it is to help us understand the type of atmosphere in which God wants us to live. He wants us to live in peace, and He knows that many times we lose our peace because we are not behaving properly in a relationship.

Work with All Your Heart

Colossians 3:23–25

Whatever you do, work at it with all your heart, as working for the Lord, not for human masters, since you know that you will receive an inheritance from the Lord as a reward. It is the Lord Christ you are serving. Anyone who does wrong will be repaid for their wrongs, and there is no favoritism.

Colossians 3:23–25 continues what Paul starts in verse 22 in that it addresses how we are to think about our work. No matter how many people may be above us on an organizational chart, we ultimately work for the Lord and are to work diligently and fervently, with all of our hearts. When we know we are working for Him instead of for other human beings, the difficult things we have to do are made easier.

We can be encouraged because Paul tells us that when we work as though we are working for God, we will be rewarded. We know that we reap what we sow (Gal. 6:7) and that good work brings good rewards. When we work to impress or satisfy other people, we may never get the rewards we hope for, such as recognition, appreciation, promotion, or a nice bonus. But when we work as though we are working for the Lord and we have good attitudes about what we are doing,

He rewards us in ways He knows will be most fulfilling and meaningful to us. It may be a bonus, an expression of gratitude, or some type of recognition, or it may be something even better.

Personal Reflection

Based on the fact that you are working for the Lord and not for other people, are there any adjustments you need to make in your attitude toward work?

Masters and Slaves

Colossians 4:1

*Masters, provide your slaves with what is right and fair,
because you know that you also have a Master in heaven.*

Certain people in Colossae employed others as slaves, and
Paul has already written to the slaves concerning how they
should behave (Col. 3:22–25). Now he reminds the masters
here that though they may be called earthly "masters," they
answer to the Master in heaven, God Himself. For this reason, Paul urges them to treat their slaves with integrity and
justice. This doesn't mean that slavery was in any way right,
but if anyone did own slaves, Paul wanted to make sure they
were treated right.

Paul understands that human societies do make distinc-
tions among people, but God does not. He writes in Galatians 3:28, "There is neither Jew nor Gentile, neither slave
nor free, nor is there male and female, for you are all one in
Christ Jesus." And in Romans 2:11, he says, "For God shows
no partiality [undue favor or unfairness; with Him one man
is not different than another]" (AMPC). In God's eyes, we are
all created equal.

Paul writes in most of his letters about how to handle various relationships in godly ways, whether they are marriage

relationships, social relationships, church relationships, or other associations—just as we saw in Colossians 3:18–22. Here, he focuses on the relationship between master and slave. We can see from this verse that he cares about the slaves' well-being. These same Scriptures can and should be applied to bosses and their employees.

Paul's epistle to Philemon is a very short book of the Bible. It is only one chapter, which pertains exclusively to the relationship between Philemon, the master, and Onesimus, a slave who ran away from him. Philemon is believed to have lived in Colossae and been a leader in the Colossian church. After Onesimus fled from Philemon's service, Onesimus met Paul, probably in Rome, and became a believer under his ministry. Paul cared about Onesimus, and he became a valuable helper to Paul (Philem. 12–13). Because Philemon was also a believer, Paul urged him to forgive Onesimus for running away and to reconcile with Onesimus and allow him to work for Philemon again—not as a slave, but as a brother in Christ (Philem. 16).

Obviously, Paul felt compassion for slaves and wanted them to be treated justly. Not only does he urge masters in general to be good to their slaves, but he also took a personal interest in the relationship between Philemon and Onesimus and worked to see the two of them rightly related to each other.

Devoted to Prayer

Colossians 4:2

Devote yourselves to prayer, being watchful and thankful.

In much of Colossians 4, Paul lays groundwork for the future of the church at Colossae, letting them know who he plans to send to help them. He also passes along greetings from other ministers. But before he reaches that point, he leaves the Colossians with practical and spiritual advice to help them mature as believers. His first instruction is to pray.

One of the best things we can do with our lives is to devote ourselves to prayer. I think some people misunderstand what prayer really is, so I'd like to clear up a few misconceptions about it. First, prayer is not an obligation; it is the greatest privilege we have. Second, prayer is not a religious activity; it is a relational conversation. If we over-spiritualize prayer and turn it into something it isn't, we will not want to pray. It does not require being in a certain place, assuming a certain posture, or using theological words in a certain tone of voice. Third, we don't have to pray for a specific length of time or at specific times of day. Prayer is simply talking with God and listening to Him as we would in a conversation with a friend. God is our friend, and He wants to interact with us just the way we are, not with us trying to seem "religious" or super spiritual. We may have special set apart times for prayer, and that is good, but keep in mind that we can pray anywhere at any time. You may want to kneel when you pray, and if so, that is good, but you can also pray while you're taking a walk.

I like to teach people to pray their way through the day. Let prayer become like breathing. Each day, start a conversation with God about anything and everything. As you go about your day, simply talk with Him about everything that happens, about the people you encounter, about what you think and how you feel. There is nothing—absolutely nothing—that is off-limits with God. If something is on your mind, you can tell Him all about it. Prayer opens the door to the power of God and invites Him to change things and people. It opens doors you could never open and closes doors that would lead to something that is not good or right for you.

Prayer is what changes our circumstances and our relationships, and it also changes us. It is amazing to pray and then watch God answer your prayers. It is one of my greatest joys in life.

There are many reasons to pray, but I want to focus on just two of them. The first reason is that God hears us when we pray, and He answers us. According to James 5:16, "The heartfelt *and* persistent prayer of a righteous man (believer) can accomplish much [when put into action and made effective by God—it is dynamic and can have tremendous power]" (AMP). The second reason we need to pray is that prayer is our first line of defense against the enemy, which means it is our first step toward victory over him.

God Hears and Answers Prayer

Some people are reluctant to pray because they do not think God will hear and answer them. Others hesitate to pray because they are independent and want to do things themselves. They fail to realize how much God loves them and wants help to them. God is interested in everything that concerns us; no matter how tiny or seemingly unimportant it may be, if it concerns us, God is interested in it. If something hurts us, God wants to comfort us. If something is too hard for us, He wants to help.

There is only one requirement related to getting help from God: we have to ask. James 4:2 says, "You do not have because you do not ask God." And Jesus says in Matthew 7:7: "Ask *and* keep on asking and it will be given to you; seek *and* keep on seeking and you will find; knock *and* keep on knocking and the door will be opened to you" (AMP). To have prayers answered, we start by asking. We may need to persevere, but eventually the door will be opened. God does hear and answer prayer (Matt. 7:8; 1 Pet. 3:12; 1 John 5:14; Ps. 91:15). Of course, there are hindrances to prayers being answered, such as unforgiveness in our hearts (Mark 11:25). If you want to learn more about things that hinder effective prayer, you will find detailed information about it in my book *The Power of Simple Prayer.*

Prayer Is Our First Line of Defense against the Enemy

1 Peter 5:8–9 says, "Be alert and of sober mind. Your enemy the devil prowls around like a roaring lion looking for someone to devour. Resist him, standing firm in the faith, because

you know that the family of believers throughout the world is undergoing the same kind of sufferings." To "be alert and of sober mind" is similar to Colossians 4:2, when it instructs us to be "watchful." I don't think anyone should be afraid of the devil, but we do need to be alert because he is actively looking for someone to destroy.

The key to resisting the enemy is to do so when he first begins to tempt or harass you. In the Amplified Bible, Classic Edition, 1 Peter 5:9 says, "Withstand him; be firm in faith [*against his onset*]" (emphasis mine). When you are alert to the enemy's schemes and tactics, then the minute he tries to attack you, you can resist. As soon as an offense comes into your heart and you feel yourself wanting to withdraw from another person, that's the moment to say, "God, help me to forgive and release this situation and get over it." The instant you find yourself feeling jealous because someone else has gotten what you want, that's the time to say, "God, I choose to rejoice with that person. Help me to be genuinely happy for them." Don't wait until negative thoughts and bad attitudes have a chance to take root in your soul, because once something is deeply rooted inside of you, getting rid of it is much more difficult. It is easier if we recognize what the enemy is doing and deal with it right away. Resist the devil at his onset!

In Colossians 4:2, Paul teaches us not only to be watchful but also to be thankful. Whenever we pray, we should do so with a thankful heart. We can thank God in advance for the way He will answer our prayers and for all the good things He has done in our lives.

Pray for Others

Colossians 4:3–4

And pray for us, too, that God may open a door for our message, so that we may proclaim the mystery of Christ, for which I am in chains. Pray that I may proclaim it clearly, as I should.

In addition to urging the Colossians to devote themselves to prayer, Paul asks them to pray for him, that he would proclaim the mystery and message of Christ clearly. He did not let the fact that he was in prison stop him from sharing his insights and encouragement with Christians in the early church. He was not free to travel and minister, but his passion for Jesus and sense of urgency about the spreading of the gospel never diminished. He continued his ministry from behind bars through writing letters. I hope that you are as thankful as I am for Paul's epistles, because each one is a treasure to us as Christians. Each one helps us understand the spiritual realities we enjoy as believers and helps us know how to live our everyday lives in ways that please God.

CHAPTER 14

THE IMPORTANCE OF ENCOURAGEMENT

Ways to Draw Others to Christ

Colossians 4:5

Be wise in the way you act toward outsiders; make the most of every opportunity.

Here Paul is talking about how Christians are to act toward non-Christians. This is extremely important because society today is filled with people who do not know Christ. At the same time, Christians are everywhere, and God wants to use us to influence non-Christians. God has placed His people everywhere. We are in businesses, we are in shopping malls, we are in schools, and we are in neighborhoods all over the world. Sometimes, we're shy about our faith or intimidated by the nonbelievers around us, but people should be able to see that we are different. But oftentimes, we blend in by behaving as nonbelievers do.

2 Corinthians 5:20 says, "So we are Christ's ambassadors, God making His appeal as it were through us. We [as Christ's personal representatives] beg you for His sake to lay hold of the divine favor [now offered you] *and* be reconciled to God" (AMPC). This Scripture really grips my heart every time I read it. Just think about it for a moment: We (you and I) are personal representatives of Christ and should behave as He would in every situation.

Have you ever thought about the fact that you may be the only representative of Jesus that the people around you will ever see? That is true, so it's no wonder Paul urges us to be wise in our interactions with them. Here are three simple suggestions you might consider when dealing with people, especially those who do not know Christ:

1. Make them feel good about themselves.

Christians have gained a reputation for being judgmental and acting superior to others, trying to make them feel worse about themselves instead of better. That kind of arrogance is not biblical at all.

You can always start with a smile. A smile can brighten up a moment and help people feel at ease very quickly. You can also say something that will put a smile on people's faces, even if it's a simple compliment about something they are wearing or the way they style their hair. They may not remember the exact words you spoke, but they will remember that you made them feel good.

2. Be peaceful and stay stable.

Have you noticed how upset, tense, and easily angered people are these days? I am sure they would like to have peace, but they have no idea how to get it. If you can be the person who stays at peace when everyone else is anxious or stressed-out, it won't be long until people start asking you why. Once they open the door by asking about it, you can simply tell them it is because you have Jesus in your life helping you at all times, and that He is available to them also.

If they accept what you say, then share as much as they are willing to hear. And if they reject what you say, just continue showing the fruit of the Holy Spirit and praying for them. In our world today, negative emotions are seen everywhere. Whether it's a child throwing a tantrum in a grocery store, a teenager sobbing to a friend in a coffee shop, or someone with road rage, the level of emotional intensity is high. People seem to be easily angered and offended.

Sometimes things affect us deeply on an emotional level for legitimate reasons, but I am talking about the out-of-control emotions some people have and the ever-changing moods they display. The Bible tells us that in the last days many will be offended and betray and hate one another (Matt. 24:10). It certainly seems those days are upon us.

If you can be the stable person in your workplace, your neighborhood, your family, or any other group, people will notice. They will pay attention when you stay calm while everyone is upset. Circumstances should not be in control of your emotions. With God's help, you can control them. You can stay steady when everyone else is tossed about emotionally because of things that happen. My husband's stability is one of the main things that prompted me to want to go deeper in God and find the peace I saw demonstrated in his life.

3. Value people.

Many people today do not feel special, loved, or valued at all. As Christians, we know the opposite is true. Everyone is precious to God, and showing that we value them is one of the best things we can do for them. There are many simple ways to show people they are important, such as expressing interest in the things they are interested in, taking time to listen and be compassionate when they need to vent about a problem, meeting a practical need in their lives, sitting with them at lunch or asking how they are during a break at work, and showing sympathy and support if they are going through a difficult time. Helping people feel valued does not require a lot of time, money, or effort, yet it still makes a significant impact on them.

In addition, I would encourage you to pray and regularly ask God to give you wisdom when dealing with non-believers and to help you make the most of every opportunity you have with them. They are people He dearly loves, and you never know when He might use you to make an eternal difference in their lives.

Personal Reflection

In what practical ways can you be a good ambassador, or representative, for Christ to the people around you, especially those who do not know Him? In what ways can you come up higher in the ministry of encouragement?

_____

_____

_____

_____

_____

_____

_____

Speak Graciously

Colossians 4:6

Let your conversation be always full of grace, seasoned
with salt, so that you may know how to answer everyone.

Following Paul's instructions about how to relate to unbelievers is this verse about letting our conversation be filled with
grace. This is especially important when we are talking with
those who do not know Christ, but it's also good advice for
other conversations we may have. Gracious words are sooth-
ing and comforting. They build up instead of tearing down,
they encourage instead of discourage, and very importantly,
they make people feel valued.

We should live with the awareness that our words make a
difference. They are very powerful. Proverbs 18:21 says, "The
tongue has the power of life and death, and those who love
it will eat its fruit." Our words affect other people, and they
affect us, too. Negative, depressing words will lead to a negative, depressing life. Positive, happy words will make us positive, happy people.

What we say reveals more about who we are than anything
else. Jesus says, "For the mouth speaks what the heart is full of"
(Matt. 12:34). To find out people's level of spiritual maturity, all
we need to do is listen to them. Do they gossip? Do they break

confidentiality? Is their speech full of anger or hate, or is it filled with grace? Do they talk about their problems excessively, or do they speak of God's goodness and the fact that He is in control?

We can learn a lot about people and their spiritual maturity by what they say about themselves. People who are still immature in Christ make statements like these: "I'm so stupid." "I'm ugly." "I don't do anything right." "I don't have anything to look forward to."

In contrast, people who are mature in Christ say things like this: "I have the mind of Christ, and I can do all things through Him because He gives me strength." "I am created in God's image, and He doesn't make anything ugly." "I have a hope and a future in God. Things may not be going great right now, but He has good things in store for me."

Personal Reflection

How can you replace negative thoughts and speech with truths that line up with what God says in His Word?

Paul Sends Help

Colossians 4:7–9

Tychicus will tell you all the news about me. He is a dear
brother, a faithful minister and fellow servant in the Lord.
I am sending him to you for the express purpose that
you may know about our circumstances and that he may
encourage your hearts. He is coming with Onesimus, our
faithful and dear brother, who is one of you. They will tell
you everything that is happening here.

Paul begins to bring his letter to a close by telling the Colossians
what will happen next. He has chosen two people—Tychicus
and Onesimus—to send to Colossae as a means of helping
them continue to grow in Christ and to build his relationship
with the church. Since Paul is in prison in Rome while writing
Colossians, he cannot personally go to them. But he can send
others who will update them on Paul's circumstances and who
will strengthen the church in the same spirit as Paul would have.

Notice that it is important to Paul for Tychicus to encourage the hearts of the believers in Colossae. Good ministers
are able to do this, and they make it a priority. Remember,
each of us is called to minister and to be an ambassador for
Christ (2 Cor. 5:20) wherever we go. One easy way to do that
is to be an encourager—to speak an encouraging word or
lend a helping hand to everyone we meet.

Greetings and Grace

Colossians 4:10–18

My fellow prisoner Aristarchus sends you his greetings,
as does Mark, the cousin of Barnabas. (You have received
instructions about him; if he comes to you, welcome him.)
Jesus, who is called Justus, also sends greetings. These are
the only Jews among my co-workers for the kingdom of God,
and they have proved a comfort to me. Epaphras, who is
one of you and a servant of Christ Jesus, sends greetings.
He is always wrestling in prayer for you, that you may
stand firm in all the will of God, mature and fully assured.
I vouch for him that he is working hard for you and for
those at Laodicea and Hierapolis. Our dear friend Luke,
the doctor, and Demas send greetings. Give my greetings to
the brothers and sisters at Laodicea, and to Nympha and
the church in her house. After this letter has been read to
you, see that it is also read in the church of the Laodiceans
and that you in turn read the letter from Laodicea. Tell
Archippus: "See to it that you complete the ministry you
have received in the Lord." I, Paul, write this greeting in my
own hand. Remember my chains. Grace be with you.

Greetings in Paul's day were not as casual as they are today.
As I mentioned in my comments on Colossians 1, New

Testament greetings were more powerful than the ones people exchange in the modern world. I think they were also more intentional. Paul not only offers the equivalent of "Luke says hello," but also takes time to comment on each person who sends a greeting and to explain who each person is, what they mean to him, or why they are valuable to the Colossians (such as Epaphras, because of the way he prays for them).

Paul also asks the Colossians to send his letter to the church at Laodicea when they have finished reading it and to read the letter from Laodicea. Remember, in his day, people could not send emails or text messages; they had to rely on letters that were delivered by hand. There were no scanners or copy machines, so duplicating a letter would have been very time-consuming. The most efficient way for Paul to continue to minister even though he was in prison was for churches to share his letters with one another.

Paul opens this letter by wishing the Colossians grace and peace, and his last words to them are similar: "Grace be with you" (Col. 4:18). Paul understood the importance of believers receiving God's grace, and he concludes his message with this blessing, pronouncing God's undeserved favor and supernatural, enabling power to them once again.

I can just imagine how it thrilled the Colossians to receive Paul's letter, and I hope you are just as thrilled to have this book on Colossians. You have the same letter that the Colossians received, and all of its instructions apply to us today just as they did to those who first read this epistle. A large part of this letter is aimed at helping and encouraging the believers to know that they are in Christ and what that means. He encourages them to continue growing in Him and being formed into His image, and that is my prayer for you.

Do you have a real relationship with Jesus?

God loves you! He created you to be a special, unique, one-of-a-kind individual, and He has a specific purpose and plan for your life. And through a personal relationship with your Creator—God—you can discover a way of life that will truly satisfy your soul.

No matter who you are, what you've done, or where you are in your life right now, God's love and grace are greater than your sin—your mistakes. Jesus willingly gave His life so you can receive forgiveness from God and have new life in Him. He's just waiting for you to invite Him to be your Savior and Lord.

If you are ready to commit your life to Jesus and follow Him, all you have to do is ask Him to forgive your sins and give you a fresh start in the life you are meant to live. Begin by praying this prayer...

Lord Jesus, thank You for giving Your life for me and forgiving me of my sins so I can have a personal relationship with You. I am sincerely sorry for the mistakes I've made, and I know I need You to help me live right.

Your Word says in Romans 10:9, "If you declare with your mouth, 'Jesus is Lord,' and believe in your heart that God raised him from the dead, you will be saved" (NIV). I believe You are the Son of God and confess You as my Savior and Lord. Take me just as I am, and work in my heart, making me the person You want me to be. I want to live for You, Jesus, and I am so grateful that You are giving me a fresh start in my new life with You today.

I love You, Jesus!

It's so amazing to know that God loves us so much! He wants to have a deep, intimate relationship with us that grows every day as we spend time with Him in prayer and Bible study. And we want to encourage you in your new life in Christ.

Please visit **joycemeyer.org/knowJesus** to request Joyce's book *A New Way of Living*, which is our gift to you. We also have other free resources online to help you make progress in pursuing everything God has for you.

Congratulations on your fresh start in your life in Christ! We hope to hear from you soon.

ABOUT THE AUTHOR

Joyce Meyer is one of the world's leading practical Bible teachers. A *New York Times* bestselling author, Joyce's books have helped millions of people find hope and restoration through Jesus Christ. Joyce's programs, *Enjoying Everyday Life* and *Everyday Answers with Joyce Meyer*, air around the world on television, radio, and the Internet. Through Joyce Meyer Ministries, Joyce teaches internationally on a number of topics with a particular focus on how the Word of God applies to our everyday lives. Her candid communication style allows her to share openly and practically about her experiences so others can apply what she has learned to their lives.

Joyce has authored more than one hundred books, which have been translated into more than one hundred languages, and over 65 million of her books have been distributed worldwide. Bestsellers include *Power Thoughts*; *The Confident Woman*; *Look Great, Feel Great*; *Starting Your Day Right*; *Ending Your Day Right*; *Approval Addiction*; *How to Hear from God*; *Beauty for Ashes*; and *Battlefield of the Mind*.

Joyce's passion to help hurting people is foundational to

the vision of Hand of Hope, the missions arm of Joyce Meyer Ministries. Hand of Hope provides worldwide humanitarian outreaches such as feeding programs, medical care, orphanages, disaster response, human trafficking intervention and rehabilitation, and much more—always sharing the love and Gospel of Christ.

JOYCE MEYER MINISTRIES

U.S. & FOREIGN OFFICE ADDRESSES

Joyce Meyer Ministries
P.O. Box 655
Fenton, MO 63026
USA
(636) 349-0303

Joyce Meyer Ministries—Canada
P.O. Box 7700
Vancouver, BC V6B 4E2
Canada
(800) 868-1002

Joyce Meyer Ministries—Australia
Locked Bag 77
Mansfield Delivery Centre
Queensland 4122
Australia
(07) 3349 1200

Joyce Meyer Ministries—England
P.O. Box 1549
Windsor SL4 1GT
United Kingdom
01753 831102

Joyce Meyer Ministries—South Africa
P.O. Box 5
Cape Town 8000
South Africa
(27) 21-701-1056

Other Books by Joyce Meyer

The Power of Being Thankful
The Power of Determination
The Power of Forgiveness
The Power of Simple Prayer
Power Thoughts
Power Thoughts Devotional
Reduce Me to Love
The Secret Power of Speaking God's Word
The Secrets of Spiritual Power
The Secret to True Happiness
Seven Things That Steal Your Joy
Start Your New Life Today
Starting Your Day Right
Straight Talk
Teenagers Are People Too!
Trusting God Day by Day
The Word, the Name, the Blood
Woman to Woman
You Can Begin Again
Your Battles Belong to the Lord*

Joyce Meyer Spanish Titles

Belleza en Lugar de Cenizas (*Beauty for Ashes*)
Buena Salud, Buena Vida (*Good Health, Good Life*)
Cambia Tus Palabras, Cambia Tu Vida (*Change Your Words, Change Your Life*)
El Campo de Batalla de la Mente (*Battlefield of the Mind*)
Como Formar Buenos Habitos y Romper Malos Habitos (*Making Good Habits, Breaking Bad Habits*)
La Conexión de la Mente (*The Mind Connection*)
Dios No Está Enojado Contigo (*God Is Not Mad at You*)

La Dosis de Aprobación (The Approval Fix)
Efesios: Comentario Biblico (Ephesians: Biblical Commentary)
Empezando Tu Día Bien (Starting Your Day Right)
Hazte Un Favor a Ti Mismo...Perdona (Do Yourself a Favor...Forgive)
Madre Segura de sí Misma (The Confident Mom)
Pensamientos de Poder (Power Thoughts)
Sanidad para el alma de una mujer (Healing the Soul of a Woman)
Santiago: Comentario bíblico (James: Biblical Commentary)
Sobrecarga (Overload)*
Sus batallas son del Señor (Your Battles Belong to the Lord)
Termina Bien Tu Día (Ending Your Day Right)
Usted Puede Comenzar de Nuevo (You Can Begin Again)
Viva Valientemente (Living Courageously)
*Study Guide available for this title

Books by Dave Meyer

Life Lines